The Passage of a
PICTURE BRIDE

The Passage of a
PICTURE BRIDE

Won K. Yoon

PacificRim Press
Loma Linda, California

"Picture Bride" from *Picture Bride* by Cathy Song (New Haven:
Yale University Press, 1983) reprinted with the permission of
Yale University Press. "Declaration of Independence" from
Robert T. Oliver, *Syngman Rhee: The Man Behind the Myth*
(New York: Dodd Mead Co., 1954), reprinted with the
permission of Dodd Mead Co.

Cataloging in Publication Data
Yoon, Won Kil
        The Passage of Picture Bride
        1. Chung Young Oak. 2. Korean Americans-Biography.
I. Title.
E184.K6Y6   973.004957

Library of Congress Catalog Card Number: 91-77227
ISBN 0-944450-11-3
Printed in the U.S.A.

PacificRim Press
P.O. Box 1066
Loma Linda, CA 92354
Tel (909) 796-4252
Fax (909) 792-3133

Mrs. Chung Young Oak (1988)

Miss Lee Young Oak before departure as a picture bride (1918)

Dedicated to

Mrs. Chung Young Oak,
Other Korean Picture Brides,
Their Children, and
Their Children's Children

Contents

PICTURE BRIDE

by Cathy Song

She was a year younger
than I,
twenty-three when she left Korea.
Did she simply close
the door of her father's house
and walk away. And
was it a long way
through the tailor shops of Pusan
to the wharf where the boat
waited to take her to an island
whose name she had
only recently learned,
on whose shore
a man waited,
turning her photograph
to the light when the lanterns
in the camp outside
Waialua Sugar Mill were lit
and the inside of his room
grew luminous
from the wings of moths
migrating out of the cane stalks?
What did my grandmother
take with her? And when
she arrived to look
into the face of the stranger
who was her husband,
thirteen years older than she,
did she politely untie
the silk bow of her jacket
her tent-shaped dress
filling with the dry wind
that blew from the surrounding fields
where the men were burning the cane?

—from PICTURE BRIDE (1983)

PREFACE

I happened to be introduced to Mrs. Chung Young Oak in September, 1985, while I was conducting library research at the East-West Center and at the University of Hawaii, Honolulu. One evening she invited me to a dinner and, in the course of the evening hours, she shared with me some of her early experiences in Hawaii. I instantly recognized the value of her life story. In fact, I became more interested in the fascinating story of Mrs. Chung than the research project on hand. It was a case of serendipity in every sense of the word.

When I found she was approaching eighty-five years of age, I worried about the possible loss of her rare story, either due to a sudden memory loss or worse. Yet, I had to leave Honolulu on the scheduled return date to be ready for the fall quarter at Loma Linda University.

As soon as the school year ended in June of the following year, I went back to Honolulu and recorded her entire story. Contrary to my worry, Mrs. Chung was strong and alert, with an amazing photographic memory as she recalled most events without difficulty. The octogenarian still remembered names, dates, and even contents of many interesting conversations. In many instances, she appeared to go back to the scenes of 60 or 70 years ago and relive them. She laughed, cried, and trembled as she recalled the past. The lady was a wonderful story-teller.

She told her life story in Korean, but I decided to write it in English. Primarily I wanted to share the story with the younger generation Koreans in America who may not fully understand the roots of their past. They include Mrs. Chung's children, grandchildren, and great grandchildren. Now the Chung clan numbers more than 100. Also, the decision to publish her story in English was based upon my impression that a great many of the highly-educated Koreans in Korea and abroad might be able to read it in English. But the story is for everyone. All people will enjoy reliving this story of a very amazing person. One does not have to be Korean to be inspired by this life.

I carried a full load of teaching and other responsibilities while preparing the manuscript. Since I worked during the odd hours of my weekly schedule, the progress was disappointingly slow. But my wish to hand to Mrs. Chung the story in print, perhaps her last dream in this life, kept me going.

There are many deserving my gratitude. First of all, I am thankful to Mrs. Chung for her enthusiasm and willing cooperation with the project. She endured many hours of interview, sometimes recorded six hours a day with only brief breaks. When the English manuscript was ready for her review, she volunteered to come to Loma Linda and spend almost a week. The July temperature of the San Bernardino Valley hovered over 100 degrees during the daytime, but she endured the heat and the slow process of review through a reverse translation—from English into Korean. During the review, Walter Chung and his wife kept the house cool and took care of other needs. Pastor Charles Moon of the Honolulu Korean Adventist Church volunteered his service for the collection of old documents and pictures included in this volume. Besides this, he spent many hours taking care of my needs away from home. Mr. Frank F. Fasi, the Mayor of Honolulu, and Mr. Donald O. Bieber, of Castle Medical Center, kindly supplied the information I asked for. The comments of Dr. Karen

Leonard at the University of California, Irvine, were ex-tremely valuable in improving the manuscript. Also Ruth Davis helped a lot during the improvement of the manuscript. But without the support of Loma Linda University, I could not have launched the research project in the first place. In addition, when I approached Dr. Bailey Gillespie, the director of Loma Linda University Press, with a sample chapter of the draft, he recognized the value of the story and encouraged me to submit the entire manuscript. From that point on, he guided every step in the preparation of the manuscript. It is significant, I be-lieve, that the life story of Mrs. Chung has been published by the Loma Linda University Press, because two of her sons and many of her grandchildren are graduates of the university.

Finally, my wife, Choon Ja, and two children, Tim and Christine, kept prodding and encouraging me with firm-ness and kindness. They understood my excuses for miss-ing many social occasions and family responsibilities. It is my hope that this book will both inspire, encourage, and retell a very significant story.

Won Kil Yoon
Riverside,1989

INTRODUCTION

The story of Mrs. Chung Young Oak is one of more than 1,000 Korean picture brides who left their country between 1910 and 1924.1 By now, most of the picture brides have passed away, and the surviving few are in their 80's and 90's. Many of their stories, perhaps far more sad than happy, are buried in the graves of the deceased and in the dim memory of the surviving ones.

It is possible that the formidable language barrier kept the mothers and grandmothers from telling their stories to their children and grandchildren. It is also quite possible that many Korean picture brides who were brought up in the culture of shame didn't want to reveal their pitiful life stories.

Even if there was no language barrier, the early Korean immigrants would not have had the latitude of mind to share their experiences with their offsprings. They had far more pressing concern than transmitting their life in speech or writing. Survival was constantly haunting them. In addition to the difficulties of this new life, about 60 percent of the early Korean immigrants were illiterate.2

At the same time, the paucity of writings on the life of early immigrants may be attributed to the orientation of the few Korean writers. They were educated in America during the early decades of this century and published works in English.3 Yet they did not pay literary attention to the predicaments of their fellow countrymen. Their upper-class, aristocratic upbringing made it difficult to identify with common laborers. Instead, they were more concerned about assimilation into American culture. They saw their roles in America as cultural ambassadors of goodwill or tour guides.4 Furthermore, autobiographical writing and popular fiction were not in the tradition of the Asian cultures that produced the first immigrants.5

This reluctance created a vacuum between the picture-bride generation and subsequent generations. Recently, there have been efforts to collect the histories of the early Asian immigrants, including picture brides.6 Those histories related to picture brides, however, are usually no more than compilations of brief individual recollections focused on the events around the picture marriage. Usually such fragmentary stories do not detail the backgrounds of women before picture marriages and the ensuing life events after them. Also the detailed description of the long process, ranging from picture engagement, to voyage, and marriage in Hawaii, has been seldom told. In other words, no one has yet written the entire life story of a Korean woman who came to America as a picture bride.

Mrs. Chung has long aspired to publish her story. According to her, she approached two Korean writers years ago with a hope to publish her biography in Korean, but that did not materialize. In the process she lost some of the written material that she left with the writers who failed to return it. The strong desire to publish her story has stemmed from the following considerations.

First of all, Mrs. Chung has regarded her life as blessed in terms of her own social achievement and her children's success. In spite of some pains and hardships she endured in the early years in Korea and Hawaii, she has always been grateful and proud.

Secondly, she values the contributions of the Korean picture brides to the building of the early Korean community in Hawaii. Thus she wants to see a proper recognition of the picture brides in the history of the Korean-Americans. One always detects in her a deep sympathy for the less fortunate picture brides whose lives often bordered on tragedy. Nonetheless, she believes that they were the unsung heroines who played the roles of wife and mother in the early Korean communities both in Hawaii and the mainland. Without their ventures into Hawaii as picture brides, perhaps the early Korean community might have become a male-dominant ethnic ghetto somewhat resembling the early Chinatowns in the West.[7] Until this day, she deeply appreciates the courage and long-suffering of the picture brides, and she is not ashamed of being identified as one of them.

Finally, she would like to see the children and grandchildren of the picture brides understand what their mothers and grandmothers had gone through. Once in a while, she has been asked by the children of her picture-bride friends about their mothers or grandmothers. Yet the language barrier kept Mrs. Chung from telling the children as much as she knows about other picture brides, let alone conveying the inner feelings of her friends. This has remained in her as a burden. Although she was far better off in later life than many of her peers, she faced the same agonies and hardships. She wanted to see the stories of picture brides continuously told from generation to generation. To many Korean-Americans, that would be the story of their matrilineal roots.

Moreover, what makes her story so interesting and significant is the time and place of her life events. In other words, her personal biography has been closely intertwined with the history of her country. Born in 1901, she witnessed many drastic political changes that Korea underwent in the first half of the 20th century: the fall of the last Yi Dynasty (1910), the colonization of Korea by Japan (1910-1945), the overseas independence movements during colonial rule, the liberation of Korea at the end of World War II (1945), the division along the 38th parallel (1945), the birth of the First Korean Republic (1948) led by her life-long mentor, Dr. Rhee Syngman, the Korean War (1950-1953), Reconstruction, the collapse of the First Republic (1960), and so forth.

During the turmoils, not only was her fate affected by that of her country, but also her life contributed to Korean history. Her own story may not be unusual if it is told apart from the story of struggling Korea during her life time, but she was more than a wife of a sugar-plantation laborer. Her associations with the influential figures of the independence movement based in Hawaii were not accidents. She earned respect through her commitment to Korean independence.

Thus, this book presents the life history of Mrs. Chung against the backdrop of her travailing mother country. She is presented as one of many supporting actors on the political stage of struggling Korea. It is my desire that readers may see the history of modern Korea in this personal history. The two are inseparable. The perspective taken here is what the late American sociologist C. Wright Mills called sociological imagination.[8] Realizing the constant interplay between biography and history, the meaning of one's life is to be understood in the context of a larger society.

Significance of This Study

There have been two major waves in Korean immigration to the United States. The first wave came between 1903 and 1905 when about 8,000 Koreans came to Hawaii to work on the sugar plantations of the various islands. This wave, however, lasted only a few years because of a fraud, the transporting of hundreds of Koreans to Mexico instead of the promised Hawaii. The second wave began in 1968 when the U. S. government began to implement the Immigration Amendment Act which favored the previously disfavored eastern-hemisphere countries,9 which is still hitting the shoreline of the American West coast, adding more than 20,000 Korean immigrants every year.

Between the first and second wave, there was more than half a century lapse during which only a small number of Koreans were permitted to enter the United States for permanent residence. Mostly they were the wives of returning American soldiers stationed in Korea and little orphans adopted by American families.10 Their relationship with their sponsors, either husbands or adoptive parents, made it hard to retain their ethnic identies. This has left a definite sociological disconnection between the early and late Korean communities.

However in recent years, the Korean community has become one of the fastest growing in America. Soon it may reach the first million mark. A growing community needs memories to share and stories to tell because it provides a sense of rootedness and personality. The life story of Mrs. Chung may expand the collective consciousness of Korean-Americans. At the same time, her story should bridge the early Korean immigrants and the recent arrivals. The difference in socio-economic status of the two groups is substantial, to say the least.

Another significance of her story lies in the fact that it portrays intimate accounts of the past. The majority of existing publications about the Korean Americans are mainly political (largely diplomatic), economic, educational, and religious. They are the formal, objective accounts of the state of Korean Americans at the group or community level. But a life history, such as this, may reveal the intricate aspects of a single life experience. Sometimes, subjective accounts of experience provides more indepth understanding of human existence. The subtle emotions of individual immigrants under different situations can be very enlightening.

Finally, Mrs. Chung's history for 70 years in Hawaii, spanning four generations, may serve as a good case study of the transformation among Korean immigrants. Although her own historical time and place were quite different from those of recent Korean immigrants on the mainland, the experience of her clan may give some clue about the future of many Korean families in America.

Methodology

Life history, as a means of collecting social data, is not so popular as the survey or other methods in American sociology. The overriding concern for quantifiable data and its generalizability to a wider population has led many sociologists to shun the subjective case study approach. However, there have been a few who recognize the value of life history as a means of reconstructing social reality from within.

The three central features of the life history are the person's own story of his or her life, the social and cultural situation to which the subject and others see the subject responding, and the sequence of past experiences and situations in the subject's life.[11] Using personal experience of the subject helps describe the temporal sequences of events, the social context in which they occurred, their interpretation by the subject, and how all this led him or her to believe and behave.[12] In brief, it is to uncover the effects of external events upon the internal experience of the individual.[13] The structure of the life history may be compared to a two-story house with the objective world on the ground floor and the individual's experience of that world on the second floor.[14]

The Polish Peasant in Europe and *America*, by W. I. Thomas and F. Znaniecki, was a monumental work based upon the life histories of Polish immigrants in America. This book is especially pertinent because it deals with the adjustment and transformation of the Polish immigrants in America.

Mrs. Chung's story is an 'edited life history'. Its key feature is the continual interspersing of comments, explanations, and questions by someone other than the focal subject.15 This means that I did not transcribe every word uttered by Mrs. Chung; instead I excercised my judgment in editing her story.

I let Mrs. Chung tell her story according to her recollection and perception of events. The only suggestion I made to her was the chronological order she should follow. Using a tape recorder kept disruptions to the minimum and allowed for questioning, clarification, and elaboration. While her narration was recorded by the machine, I carefully observed her paralanguage, such as the tone of the voice, body gesture, acclamation, and the like. These conveyed her mood vividly as she relived past events.

In transcribing her story, my editing was considerable. First of all, I had to translate her story into English. Much of the translation was in the form of paraphrase, except for what is directly quoted. My paraphrase, however, only involved expression, not content. There are Korean phrases the literal translation of which would sound awkward. Some of the Korean words she used were not familiar to me, especially technical terms. For instance, the word she used for *steamer* or *hour* I had never heard of. Apparently she still uses the Korean vocabularies that were used around the turn of the century in her remote hometown in Kyung Sang province.

Secondly, some segments of her story were amplified. Often she mentioned certain events that took place outside Korea or Hawaii. Yet these events affected her perception of reality significantly. Also, such amplication was necessary because some of her own actions were a part of much larger pictures about which she had a partial and dim comprehension. So I expanded her remarks by detailing their historical backgrounds. Although this book is a person's history, I tried to avoid making it ahistorical.

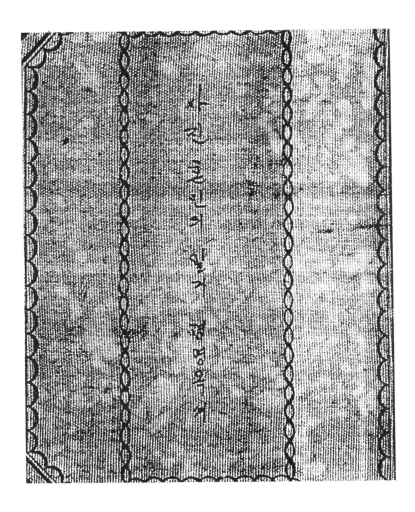

The cover of Mrs. Chung's journal on picture marriage. It reads:
Journal of Picture Marriage by Chung Young Oak

때, 못보예 소와 우신문이 본세 멋지라 며서음을 강때 가함 생각

심으로 고때용 생국오라 벼위탁 피베탁 비오 도와 국오압 무모본

어잡고 그통안 멀하나 기울이울나가 안 명하 늘나가 나운 그순간에 집

하시요 하는때울 못고 쌀미 벼가 나와 서 정봉운 새봉 는 올 내벌

남우 허보느 옥여탄 초면오씨 말이 어리나가 서두봉이 인사울

그러 줌나이본 이정봉운씨요 네그 옷육나 단나 이면 국장이 병여

씨우고 리명우 당신나이 이정봉운 씨로 맛씨기 위하더이 옷 우밧오

달이고 핫 든싯형 이용운 그렴 숩나 다앞 몃 나더로 말우 합국로

암예 해우 마런 국장 이봉오씨 말이 이 러명 옥운 기

우 뵈지 못햇 크음 어다 정봉운 씨 보녀 이민 국장

하안 요와이 통 뱃크리가 무어와 고 하반어오 그

디로 나어시요 나는 조금 건소울 쓴앗다 정봉운 씨울 거국에서 완움

A page describing the interview scene at the
immigration station in Honolulu

The author with Mrs. Chung in her apartment (above)
and recording her life story (below)

Thirdly, I did not arrange every event in a strictly chronological order. Some segments were inserted in the form of recollections or reflection. This was inevitable because of the multiplicity of life events. Even Mrs. Chung had expereinced some difficulty in following her own chronological order.

Finally, I excluded either isolated or irrelevant episodes. My decision was based on the nature of each piece in the context of the overriding theme of each chapter. I tried to present the passage of Mrs. Chung's life in a coherent manner.

Validity and Reliability

In anyone's story, there are temptations to compromise the validity and reliability of collected data. The temptations may come from either the source or the writer. The causes of such temptations may include vanity, guilt, social norms and values, the desire to please the researcher, and memory loss.

To validate some of her stories, especially the glorious parts, I collected physical evidence, such as pictures, published newspaper articles, and personal documents. For instance, her association with high Korean government officials, including the first president, is well supported by these means. Also I checked her accounts of years, names of people and places, and major events against published sources. It turned out that her memory was not clear on some of these.

In her own journals, she describes in detail some early experiences both in Korea and Hawaii. In addition, she used other sources for historical information, mainly the early Korean immigrants and a few of the Korean publications on the history of Hawaiian Koreans. She gathered fragments of personal histories from old-timers during her visits to nursing homes around Honolulu.

Unfortunately, some of the early documents, pictures, and portions of journals were lost when the family moved from the island of Maui to Honolulu. The move was made without the care of Mrs. Chung who was staying in Honolulu upon returning from Korea. She was able to reconstruct her journals, but the documents and pictures were lost forever.

Because she has told her story to others and parts of it have been published in Korean in the form of book chapters and magazine articles, I paid careful attention to any contradiction or inconsistency. I have not yet discovered any discrepancy in the stories she told to different persons.16 Whenever she detected a tinge of suspicion in me on the fidelity of her story she would tell me that she would have nothing to gain or lose by fabricating her story at her age. She was very candid about her life except for some very private segments, which she disclosed off the record.

One finds almost the quality of a novel in the life of Mrs. Chung Young Oak. From a poor sixteen-year-old picture bride to a close acquaintance of President Rhee, his wife, cabinet members, ambassadors, and military generals! From the wife of a humble sugar plantation worker to the mother of the Honolulu Police Commission chairman! If Mrs. Chung's story reads like fiction, it is because of the nature of her life events, not the style of presenting them. In spite of Norman Denzin's suggestion that, "A good life history reads like a novel."17 fictional dramatization was not attempted in this book.

I use the Korean names in the Korean way: The family names come before the given names. Also, I do not use hyphens to put the two-syllable given names together. For instance, the name of the protagonist is expressed Chung Young Oak, not Young-oak Chung. (There is no consistency among Koreans in this regard.) The English spelling of the names I use in this book may be different. (Again there is no consistency.) I tried to make the English pronounciations, however, sound as close as possible to the original sound of the Korean names.

I hope the life history of Mrs. Chung is a valuable addition to the collective story of Korean Americans in particular, and Asian Americans in general. Futhermore, this may be a worthy addition to the rich oral history of foreign immigrants in America.

NOTES

[1] Almost 1,000 picture brides joined their men in Hawaii and another 115 in California. Stephan Thernstrom (ed.) *Harvard Encyclopedia of American Ethnic groups* (Cambridge: Harvard University Press, 1980), 602.

[2] Thernstrom, 602.

[3] Early Korean writers who published in America were Kang Hyounghill and Park No-Yong. Kang's representative works include *The Grass Roof* (1931) and *East Goes West* (1937) and Parks' *An Oriental View of American Civilization* (1934) and *Retreat of the West* (1937).

[4] Elaine H. Kim, *Asian American Literature: An Introduction to the Writings and Their Social Context* (Philadelphia: Temple University Press, 1982), 32-43.

[5] Kim, 24.

[6] Maxine Hong Kingston's nonfiction bestseller *China Men* (1980) was based on the stories of early Chinese immigrants. Eileen Sunada Sarasohn collected the oral histories of the first-generation Japanese immigrants in *The Issei: Portrait of a Pioneer* (1983). Brief recollections of Japanese picture marriages, each less than a page, are presented among other subjects. See pages 106 through 114. In his book *Koreans in America* (1979) Choy Bong-youn included a chapter of oral histories of the early Korean immigrants. There is a four-page autobiography of Anna Choi who was a picture bride. The first volume of *Korean Kaleidoscope* (1982), by Sonnia Shinn Sunwoo, contains the oral history of early Korean immigrants. Sunwoo interviewed some picture brides whose stories are short and partial, less than 10 typewritten pages each.

7 The sex ratio in 1910 among the Koreans in the age bracket 20 through 49 was 13 men for each woman. After 10 years of bringing picture brides, the sex ratio was brought down to 3 men per woman. In 1930, it was 1.5 men per woman. See Tables 5 and 6 in M. Shin and D. B. Lee, *Korean Immigrants in Hawaii: A Symposium on Their Background, History, Acculturation and Public Policy Issues* (monograph) (Honolulu: University of Hawaii, 1978).

8 See the first chapter of *Sociological Imagination* by C. Wright Mills (New York: Oxford University Press, 1967).

9 A total of 7,857 Koreans came to Hawaii between 1900 and 1905, but betweem 1906 and 1910 only 45 came. The total contains 6,719 male adults, 677 female adults, and 465 children. See Table 3 in M. Shin and D. B. Lee, *Korean Immigrants in Hawaii: A Symposium on Their Background History, Acculturation and Public Policy Issues.*

10 The two groups added to about 14,000. See the section on *Korean Americans in Racial and Ethnic Groups* (3rd ed.) by Richard T. Schaefer (Glenview: Scott, Foresman and Co., 1987).

11 Norman K. Denzin, *The Research Act* (2nd ed.) (New York: Mc-Graw-Hill book Company, 1978), 218.

12 Howard Schwartz and Jerry Jacobs, *Qualitative Sociology: A Method to the Madness* (New York: The Free Press, 1979) 62.

13 Schwartz and Jacobs, 68.

14 Schwartz and Jacobs, 61.

15 Denzin, 217.

16 For example, there are two chapters about Mrs. Chung and her son, Dr. Robert Chung in *Hawaii* (2nd edition in Korean) by Charles Moon (Seoul: Signs of Times, 1986), 127-150.

17 Norman K. Denzin (ed.), *Sociological Methods: A Sourcebook* (Chicago: Aldine Publishing Co. 1970), 417.

1

PICTURE
ENGAGEMENT

It was a muggy day in July. The annual long-rain sea-son was well under way. The streets of Ham An appeared almost empty except for a few scurrying dogs and children. The men were busy working in the rice fields and women do-ing chores around their homes. That day a well-dressed old lady came to Ham An. She was on a visit to recruit picture brides for the Korean men in Hawaii. The old lady was a sort of agent working for a Korean marriage broker in Honolulu. Her service was paid on commission. A few Ham An girls had already gone to Hawaii by her arrange-ment.

Roaming the small town for picture-bride candidates, she happened to see an innocent-looking girl who was sitting, facing the street, on the wooden floor of her house. The lady stopped and quickly initiated a conversation:

"What is your name, and how old are you?"

"My name is Lee Young Oak, and I am 15 years old," the girl answered without any hesitation.

"Young Oak, would you be interested in going to America?"

"Are you Jinjoo Grandma?" Young Oak instantly knew what the old lady was up to.

"Yes," the lady replied with a quick smile. Since the match-maker lived in the nearby city of Jinjoo, the folks at Ham An called her "Jinjoo Grandma."

Quickly checking around, Young Oak whispered, "Please, let's go to a place where we can talk without being seen by others."

The lady followed Young Oak at a fast pace. The house Young Oak entered was her aunt's place, and fortunately no one was home. As soon as they sat on the floor, Young Oak inquired about America. The match-maker told Young Oak that many Korean girls were going to Hawaii to marry Korean men who were making a good living. She said she was in town to look for girls who would be picture brides.

"Grandma, I am only 15. Can I still marry?"

"Why not? Although you are 15 years old, you look at least 18. You look tall and mature for your age. Moreover, you are pretty. Whoever takes you is a lucky man." Young Oak was instantly excited about the possibility of going to America, and she volunteered to bring two neighbor girls. The match-maker couldn't be happier with the prospect of recruiting three picture brides from one visit.

As soon as she saw her neighbor girls, Young Oak screamed, "Come with me. I have good news for you."

"What is going on? Do we marry someone in America as the daughter of Mr. Koo did?" one of the two girls asked. Young Oak was surprised by her friends' question, wondering how they knew. In a few minutes, Young Oak rounded up two girls, Lee Sunhee and Yim Subi. Sunhee was 19

years old and Subi was 21. The older girls were a bit apprehensive. The match-maker turned to Subi and said. "Your
prime age for marriage is over. You better hurry to find a
man. Don't be a headache to your parents."

Young Oak, with a tinge of excitement, asked the lady to
explain to them in detail about the picture marriage.

"You girls know the respectful Mr. Koo, who is a teacher
at the Ham An Normal School. His sister went to Hawaii
not long ago and married a Korean man. Lately the family
has been receiving money and expensive clothes. If I were
you, I would definitely go to Hawaii. There no one worries
about their next meal and firewood. Moreover, if you marry
here, you become a slave to your husband and his parents
until you die. In Hawaii, no one bothers you." It was a
powerful promotion speech, and the girls began to show interest.

"Do we marry Americans?" Young Oak asked.

"No, you will marry a Korean man," the match-maker
assured her.

"Then how can we find a man in Hawaii?" Young Oak
kept asking.

"Don't worry. I will arrange everything for you. That's
my job. The only thing you have to do is to get a picture
taken. The match is made with the pictures of both sides."

"But we don't have any money to have a picture taken,"
Young Oak sounded worried.

"Remember, I arrange everything for you girls. I will
bring a Japanese photographer when you are ready."

The three girls decided to give it a try. But they had another problem. None of them had a decent dress for picture
taking. After much discussion, they decided to put on the
best silk dress of Subi's sister-in-law who recently married
her brother. To their relief, the dress fit all three of them
reasonably well.

Standing in front of a pile of golden barley sheaves, the
three girls had their picture taken one by one, each wearing
the identical Chima Jugori (a Korean woman's costume).

After the picture taking, the match-maker told the girls that it would take about sixty days to hear from her.

"I will send your pictures to my boss in Hawaii with your names and ages written on the back of the pictures. When I come back to see you, I will bring the pictures of your future husbands and money."

"Do we get money for doing this?" Young Oak asked with a big smile.

"Yes, your man will send you money," the match-maker proudly replied. The older girls pinched Young Oak for her excitement over the whole matter of a picture marriage.

The girls begged the match-maker to keep their venture secret. None of them wanted to risk losing the chance of marrying in Ham An in case the picture marriage proposal should not go through.

Young Oak's curiosity about America dated back to her Sunday school kindergarten days. When Young Oak saw the fair-looking American missionary family from the southern port city Masan visiting the Ham An Presbyterian Church for the first time, she was fascinated by the Americans. These well-dressed and well-mannered people looked like angels to her. And their halting Korean sounded like the tongue of angels. The missionary children were the object of exceeding envy. Since then, her wish to go to the fairyland of America was always on her mind. Every time she heard the magic word "America" she got excited. But the dreamland existed only in the imagination of the poor hamlet girl.

Now that paradise was almost a reality within her reach, she was happy at the prospect of going to America. She didn't care at all about the method of picture marriage. She was just overwhelmed with the idea of America.

As far as Young Oak could remember, her family had always been struggling. Her family used to live in a small house in the backyard of her maternal grandmother. Her father's silk merchant business was failing, and the family had no other source of income.

Occasionally her mother collected grains and vegetables in exchange for dress-making services. Often Young Oak saw her mother worry about the next meal. Sometimes the family skipped meals. The mother cried almost every day, thinking of her son who was barely making ends meet as a college student in Tokyo. Without any help from his family, he had to support himself. So Young Oak thought that she might be able to help her parents and her student brother in Tokyo by marrying a wealthy Korean in Hawaii.

As the Koreans say, the day of fate finally came. On a beautiful September day, the match-maker returned to Ham An and stopped at Young Oak's house. Again Young Oak took the match-maker to her aunt's house. Young Oak requested her aunt to leave them alone by suggesting that she go to her place. Young Oak didn't want anyone to know about the picture marriage plan until the final deal was made. None of the three girls wanted to jeopardize their chance to marry in Ham An in case the picture marriage deal shouldn't go through. Thus the three girls imposed a strict gag order upon themselves. The other two girls also came to see the match-maker.

"Did you bring the pictures of the men in Hawaii? The time seems to have passed so slowly," Young Oak queried impatiently.

"Of course. Not only did I bring pictures but also money." The match-maker was in a good mood. But the older girls appeared indifferent.

"Are they good-looking men?" Young Oak asked.

"I don't know. Only you girls can tell whether they are good-looking or not," the match-maker answered.

The other girls remained silent. This made the match-maker nervous. She murmured to Young Oak, "If they change their minds, I am in big trouble. I hope they stick to the promise they made."

Not hearing any particular objection from the girls, the match-maker took out three pictures from her purse. As the match-maker read anxiety in the faces of the three girls, she looked uneasy. While holding the pictures in her hand, the match-maker asked, "Do you really want to marry the men in Hawaii?"

Young Oak again responded, "Grandma, don't worry. We are just nervous. We have not discussed with our parents this important matter of marriage."

With Young Oak's assurance, the match-maker began to hand a specific picture to a specific girl according to the writing on the back of each picture.

Apparently the matches were already made by someone without the consent of the girls.

The 19-year old Sunhee was matched with a 37-year-old man and the 21-year-old Subi was matched with a 38-year-old man. The 15-year-old Young Oak was matched with the oldest of the three picture grooms. On the back of the picture handed to her Young Oak read in pencil, "My name is Chung Bong Woon, and I am 42 years old. I picked Lee Young Oak."

Without looking at the face of the man in the picture, Young Oak protested to the match-maker. "Jinjoo Grandma, how come I was matched with the 42-year-old man? Didn't you know that I am the youngest of the three? I am sure the marriage broker or the man in Hawaii mistook my picture for someone else's. Otherwise such a match could not happen." The other girls joined Young Oak in complaining that their men were too old.

With an understanding voice, the Jinjoo grandma tried to calm down her clients, "I know the men are old, but old husbands know how to treat their wives right. They went to Hawaii many years ago when there were hardly any Korean young women there. Consequently, they lost the chance to marry in their 20's and even 30's. But remember that if you girls marry these men, it will bring you and your family a great fortune."

Nevertheless, Young Oak was quite disturbed by the fact that the man she was matched with was older than her mother. She felt the irony of fate. Her mother had advised Young Oak never to marry an old man. Young Oak knew the reason for such repeated advice. Her mother had married Young Oak's father who was a widower 10 years her senior. She observed that there seemed to be no joy and happiness in the married life of her parents. It was just a duty-bound marriage.

As a matter of fact, Young Oak became more concerned about how her mother would react when the 15-year-old daughter would propose to marry a man 27 years older than herself, almost three times as old as she was.

The apprehensive match-maker told the girls that she had received 100 dollars from each man. Each would get 50 dollars (100 yen), and she would take the other 50 dollars, 30 dollars for commission and 20 dollars for the picture. The experienced match-maker told the girls to go home and take the night to think it over and come the next morning for the final decision. She didn't want to take the risk of losing both money and picture bride by paying in advance. She told the girls in a serious tone, "You girls should not take this matter lightly. If you accept the money and fail to comply with the contract, I am the one who goes to jail for the breach of contract. So take it seriously."

After the other girls left, the match-maker told Young Oak about her match with Mr. Chung Bong Woon.

"According to the letter of my broker in Honolulu, Mr. Chung is the best of the three men. The broker felt that Mr. Chung deserved the best picture bride. So he gave Mr. Chung the first choice, and he picked you from the three pictures. Not only is he a good man but also he has quite a bit of money. He is a gentleman from the Choong-chung province. Therefore, don't feel so bad about his age."

Young Oak was pleased at least to know that she was the first choice by the best man of the three.

The next morning the three girls met again with the match-maker. The older girls looked somewhat resigned.

"So did you girls have a lucky dream last night? What is your final decision?" Jinjoo Grandma's voice was mixed with appeal and anxiety.

The older girls told the match-maker that things had gone too far to change their minds. They became sympathetic with the old men who might be very disappointed if they should refuse to marry them.

They thought that receiving a picture and money from an unknown man so far away couldn't be a mere accident. It must be the work of fate. They had heard so many times the age-old Korean saying "even an old straw sandal has a matching one and chopsticks are in a matching pair."

The match-maker was relieved as the girls accepted the arrangement. Whether the girls were reluctant or not, it didn't matter. She was mainly interested in making the match deals go through and getting her commission. Although she had not seen the married life of the girls she helped match, she strongly believed that the worst marriage in Hawaii couldn't be worse than the average marriage in Korea.

From her hand bag, she took out 100 dollars and gave 50 dollars to each of the older girls. She told Young Oak that she had not received money yet from Mr. Chung but that she should hear from him soon. Before leaving Ham An, the match-maker gave final instructions to the girls. "Don't forget to write to your men in Hawaii as often as you can until you leave Korea. Good luck with your marriages in Hawaii."

The Letter from Hawaii

Young Oak didn't feel any particular emotion toward her future husband. In the picture, he looked slim but stern. His crew-cut and mustache made him look strong-willed. The only question she had was why he took the picture seated. She hoped that nothing was physically wrong with the man.

The two girls who received money were supposed to write a letter to their men, but they didn't quite know how to write a letter, let alone a love letter. Blaming Young Oak for luring them into this picture marriage, they demanded she write letters for them.

Of the three, Young Oak was best qualified for letter-writing. She had attended a church-run night school for four years and a Japanese-run normal school for two years (second grade). Furthermore, Young Oak was familiar with the Korean romantic style. Many nights during the winter months, Young Oak had been asked to read romantic novels to her widowed aunt and other ladies in the neighborhood. From this experience, she had memorized a number of romantic expressions.

Yet the three girls were struggling as to how the letter should begin. They thought beginning the letter with "Mr." didn't sound quite right for their future husbands. Finally the expression "Dear" dawned upon Young Oak. So Young Oak wrote two letters for her friends. She had a hard time trying to make them different so that the common authorship would not be discovered in case the two men should read each other's letter.

Since Young Oak didn't receive either letter or money from Mr. Chung, she had no obligation to write to him. But Young Oak jotted a few words in a piece of window paper. It was almost like a business letter. It read, "I am still waiting for your money and letter." The folded note "To Mr. Chung Bong Woon" was enclosed in one of her friend's letters.

As each day passed by, Young Oak began to feel some affection toward the man in the picture. She kept his picture at the bottom of her cloth basket, and every morning she took it out to look at. After so many picture encounters, Young Oak, who had no knowledge of kissing from printed or real-life sources, began to touch her lips to those of the picture groom. (She learned that the affectionate act was called "kiss" after she came to Hawaii.)

As time passed by, the age of Mr. Chung and his sitting position didn't bother Young Oak anymore. Even if he turned out to be an old lame, she would still marry him. The fact that he was living in America and had a lot of money made other conditions almost insignificant as far as she was concerned.

Because she looked precocious and tall for her age, match-makers had frequently submitted names of men to her parents since she was twelve. One time, she was introduced to a rich farmer who offered a piece of rice paddy and 100 yen to the parents of a girl who would marry him. He was married, but his wife could not bear him a son. So the rich man was looking for a girl who would bear him sons. Young Oak was interested in the offer for her family. She changed her mind when she saw so many women (his mother, wife, and sisters) in the same house that she might have to serve.

Believing the Korean saying that "when a magpie sings on a tree, good news comes to one's house," she checked every morning to see if a magpie would sing on the mulberry tree in her backyard.

Then, one afternoon around three, she heard a magpie singing frantically on the mulberry tree. That lucky omen triggered her excitement that good news might come from Mr. Chung. Young Oak took out the picture of Mr. Chung and whispered to it, "I will get a letter from you today."

To make sure the letter got into her hands and no one else's, she stayed around the house with her eyes constantly watching the road leading to her place.

Around four o'clock in the afternoon, the mailman came to Young Oak's house and asked her if she was going to America. Then he handed a letter from Hawaii to Young Oak. The letter came exactly on the 52nd day since the match-maker left Ham An.

Young Oak's heart was beating fast and her hands were trembling. She ran to the backyard and opened the letter. There was a 50-dollar check in a folded letter. The tone of the letter was a bit apologetic about the delay. It was a report of facts rather than a love letter, not to say a marriage proposal.

According to the letter, he had given the broker in Honolulu 100 dollars and a letter for his picture bride. When he received Young Oak's note enclosed in the letter of Mr. Kim Byung Chul, he found out that the broker had used the money and held the letter. He sincerely asked her to understand the delay and promised to write to her often and send more money later. Upon receiving a letter from a man for the first time in her life, she seemed to feel the heat of love.

It was November 1917.

The Announcement of Picture Engagement

Until this time, no one in the family knew about the picture exchange. Young Oak felt that the time had come to announce her picture engagement. So, on the same day she received the letter and money from Mr. Chung, she decided to disclose the whole matter to her parents after supper.

As soon as supper was over, Young Oak told her parents that she had something important to tell them.

"Father and mother, I have decided to go to America to marry a Korean man. The match-making has already been made."

"What kind of joke is this by a 16-year-old girl? Do you know how far away America is?" the disbelieving mother questioned.

Young Oak had never traveled even 20 miles away from home to say nothing of crossing the ocean. Furthermore, her mother was upset that such an important once-in-a-life-time decision was made without consulting her parents.

Young Oak's father remained silent as if he knew what his daughter was talking about. He sat puffing the long bamboo smoke pipe.

Young Oak showed the 50-dollar check and the picture of Mr. Chung as proof.

When the mother saw the physical evidence of her daughter's engagement, she burst into uncontrollable crying.

"Oh, my poor little one, I know why you did this. You decided to go to a foreign country and marry a strange man to help your impoverished family. This is a condemnable sin of your parents. I know you want to become a sacrifice for your family."

Even the jubilant Young Oak could not hold her tears. She cried not because she had to leave home but because her mother would be so saddened by losing her oldest daughter to a stranger in a faraway country. All the while, her father didn't say a word either approving or disapproving his daughter's picture engagement.

"The time of isolation among nations is over," finally he broke his silence. "Nowadays most countries open their doors and people travel extensively. No country is too far away to visit. I think Young Oak did the right thing."

Contrary to what Young Oak had anticipated, her father praised his daughter's decision. She was relieved to hear her father's approval of the picture engagement. Also sensing that her mother was reluctantly accepting the truth, Young Oak tried to comfort her.

"Mother, bless my marriage instead of being upset about it. I don't want to see you cry so hard about this. Although I go to a faraway country, I can visit home any time if I wish. If I marry someone here in Ham An, what is my chance to find a man with wealth and a good reputation. As you know, being a daughter of a poor family with little education, I will repeat the same hardship you have gone through. So try to see my marriage in a positive light."

Young Oak handed the check to her mother telling her that it was equivalent to 100 yen. Her mother was surprised at the amount. Young Oak assured her mother that Mr. Chung would send more money.

That night, Young Oak took out the picture of Mr. Chung and made a marriage vow. Looking straight at the picture, Young Oak whispered, "Master Chung, thank you so much for your support of my family. I will never, never forget my gratitude for your generosity. I shall be your faithful wife until my death." All the while tears of gratitude were flowing down her cheeks.

The following day, her mother bought a half dozen bags of rice and bundles of firewood with the money she cashed at the post office. At no other time in her marriage, could Young Oak's mother spend so much at one time. The mother began to appreciate what Young Oak had done for the family.

So grateful for the money she received, Young Oak wrote a letter on a two-foot long paper scroll. She repeatedly thanked Mr. Chung for his support of her family and the promise to continue to do so.

In a letter responding to the letter, Mr. Chung asked Young Oak to stop thanking him for the money he sent for his future wife's family. He said that he did simply what he had to do. Young Oak wrote once a week, and Mr. Chung replied twice a month.

Through the police station, the exit procedure began. In the ensuing months, Mr. Chung sent checks of different amounts totaling 850 dollars (1,700 yen). This was a very impressive amount of money in that small rural town. The sudden wealth had become the topic of conversation among many in Ham An.

One day the local Japanese newspaper reported the story under the heading, "Lee Young Oak Sold to Hawaii for Money." This angered her parents, especially the mother, but Young Oak didn't bother about it at all. To the disturbed mother, Young Oak said, "Mother, never mind what others say about me. Only time will tell the truth."

Not long after the newspaper report, the Ham An police station notified Young Oak to deposit the last check she received from Mr. Chung. According to a Japanese constable, the required deposit was to assure that the picture bride would keep the marriage promise. He said that some women had changed their minds after receiving a considerable amount of money from their picture grooms, thus dishonoring the subjects of the Japanese Emperor. The insolent constable contradicted himself when he said in a disgusted manner, "I don't understand you picture brides. I have heard many horrible stories about picture marriages. Many of the men in Hawaii are too old to take care of their own personal hygiene. Can't you find a decent man here in Ham An?"

Young Oak was angered by the constable's remarks. They added to the insults aimed at her by the local newspaper report. Not able to restrain herself, she blurted out, "Whether I marry an old man here in Ham An or Hawaii, that is none of your business. Please treat me the way you are supposed to do as a civil servant." The unexpected retort silenced the arrogant constable.

Somehow this incident was reported in a Seoul newspaper. Young Oak was not aware of it until her brother in Seoul inquired about it. (To this day, she cannot figure out how the local incident was reported by a Seoul newspaper.)

One day, the Ham An police station informed the three girls that they were ready to obtain a visa from the American embassy in Seoul. When they went to the American embassy, the country girls were amazed by the size of the embassy building and the number both of American and Korean employees. Furthermore, everyone spoke in English. This was a foretaste of America. A Korean translator presented the pictures of the men in Hawaii and other documents the girls had brought to the American officer in charge of issuing the visa. As they were examining the pictures and documents, the two men kept laughing. The girls could not figure out why they were laughing because they spoke in English. Then the Korean translator asked the girls why they wanted to go to America. Again Young Oak volunteered, "We go to America to marry the Korean men who went there years ago. Our documents should indicate what I am telling you." He translated it in English.

After this interview, the Korean translator brought out coffee and cake on a tray. Young Oak didn't know what the drink was. When she sipped the black-color drink, it tasted bitter. The translator told her to put sugar in it. Not knowing how to treat the cake, she put a piece of cake in the coffee cup. Soon it bloated and coffee spilled over the brink. The Korean translator quickly ate the coffee-soaked cake. Young Oak felt so ashamed. She kept her head down. She was glad no American was around the group.

Two other Korean employees in the embassy told her negative things about the men in Hawaii. They even suggested that Young Oak should change her mind. Young Oak could not understand why people were so negative about her marriage to a Korean plantation worker in Hawaii. She wondered whether the employees were jealous about her going to Hawaii.

Back at home, Young Oak began to prepare for her new life in Hawaii. She asked Mr. Koo, the teacher at the Ham An Normal School, for private English lessons, which he gladly agreed to offer.

He taught Young Oak basic English words. The first English words she learned were "husband," "wife," "thank you," and "excuse me." Soon she added other everyday English words such as "I," "you," "house," "man," "woman," "money," "good bye," and so forth. She memorized the words quickly and was taught the English alphabet and how to pronounce the letters. She took private lessons an hour a day for two months. The addition of scores of English words made her a multi-lingual person: Korean, Japanese, and English.

Young Oak was excited at the prospect of living in her dreamland. Learning the strange language seemed to assure her that going to America was real, not merely imaginary.

2

VOYAGE TO HAWAII

As the day of Young Oak's departure approached, her mother tried to turn her mind from thoughts of the impending separation. But to her disappointment, there was not much else to think about.

Nonetheless, Young Oak's mother managed to make a half dozen Chima Jugoris for Young Oak, using different fabrics and colors. If her daughter were to marry in Ham An, she would have ordered at least one dresser and made five pairs of silk quilts stuffed with cottons. But Young Oak could take only so much with her. Mr. Chung repeatedly advised his picture bride not to bring much. He said in the letters that the different climate and customs of Hawaii would make them almost useless.

Young Oak's mother really missed the hectic wedding preparations. Although the family was poor, she would rather have been in heavy debt. Since Young Oak was the first daughter, her wedding would have been a great event for the family.

It was the custom for the bride's family to prepare food and drink for hundreds of wedding guests. In the countryside, the wedding celebration, often lasting for days, was an open feast for the entire village. No one had heard of selective invitations. During the celebration, any stranger could stop by and ask for food and drink.

The bride's parents wanted to express gratitude to the family of the groom for taking their daughter. Furthermore, they wanted to impress the family of their daughter's husband with sizable wedding gifts and a feast. The initial impression affected the way the husband's family treated their daughter, and the wedding was the last long-term investment for their daughter's well-being.

At the same time, the wedding marked the separation of the daughter from her family and registered her as a permanent member of her husband's family. Koreans say that a married daughter is no less than an outsider. Parents tell their daughters that even the ghost of a dead daughter belongs to her husband's family. They say this not because they want to be rid of their grown-up daughter, but rather because they want to stress time and again that marriage requires undivided loyalty and absolute obedience to the family of one's husband. Divorce represents the most shameful dishonor a married daughter brings upon her parents. Sometimes parents refuse to let a daughter who has been rejected by her husband and his parents set foot in their home.

The picture marriage first invented by the early Chinese and Japanese immigrants defied time-honored Korean customs. Young Oak's mother would not worry about any of the expectations and rejections. Yet this left Young Oak's mother with an indescribable void in her mind.

Finally, the day came. Young Oak was supposed to go with the two other girls she had induced to the picture marriage. But one failed the eye-disease examination, and the other had not received passage money from Hawaii. Young Oak could not wait indefinitely.

Young Oak was to leave Ham An for the southern port city of Pusan via Masan to take a ship to Yokohama, Japan. Coincidentally, the departing day was the market day in Ham An, which was held every five days. Many people came from the nearby villages to the market to sell anything of value and buy the things they needed. Once every five days, the town was in a festive mood as the folks passed the time shopping and chatting. But that market day was not a happy one because one of the Ham An girls was leaving for Hawaii.

Many people came to say "good bye" to Young Oak. Without exception, the women wiped tears as they left the gate of Young Oak's house. No matter how beautiful and abundant Hawaii might be, the poor little girl was leaving her parents and hometown. They compared Young Oak to the legendary girl, Shim Chung, who was sold for her blind father. The price of her sacrifice was 300 bags of refined rice paid by sea-going merchants. Such a comparison made Young Oak and her family more sad.

According to the tale, Shim Chung left her widower father alone with rice that would be offered to Buddha to open her father's eyes. During the voyage to China, the merchants threw Shim Chung into the deep sea when they met a severe storm. The sacrifice of Shim Chung was meant to appease the angry sea god, and he was so deeply moved by the young woman's act that he sent her back to earth aboard a beautiful lotus. A few days later, the floating flower was found by fishermen who forwarded it to the king. One day the king discovered a beautiful woman in the flower, and he made Shim Chung his queen. But Shim Chung never forgot her poor blind father who lived all alone somewhere in the kingdom. At the request of the queen, the king dispatched his soldiers throughout his kingdom to find her father, but they could not locate him. Then the king decided to throw a special party for every blind man in his kingdom. On the party day, Shim Chung checked every blind man, but her father had not shown up. The party was almost over when Shim Chung's father appeared in terrible condition. Shim Chung recognized him, but he could not see her. He desperately wanted to see his daughter. This anxious desire made his eyes miraculously open, and there-after father and daughter lived happily in the palace.

As the women left Young Oak's house, they murmured, "the little Shim Chung is going to Hawaii for the poor family." But they were not sure if Young Oak would ever return to see her parents.

Young Oak's mother could hardly control her emotions as she packed things for her daughter's long journey. She was saddened that her daughter's fate would be the same as hers. She had warned her not to marry a man much older than herself. Also, she had cautioned her many times not to marry a widower. Neither of the two warnings had been heeded. But the young picture bride was not so sad as her parents. Inside she felt relief. She never wanted to marry a peasant boy from the other side of the hill, nor tread the same path as other women she had seen. She thought she had been cut out for a better lot than that of a village peas-ant wife. Yet she was careful not to show any trace of her inner satisfaction while others were expressing sorrow for her.

A horse-driven wagon was ready to take her. After em-bracing her crying mother with a few words of comfort, she boarded the wagon. Young Oak felt numb as she left her hometown. She was anxious to get to the unfamiliar land and meet the unmet future husband.

As the waving people and familiar houses slowly faded from view, all of a sudden the reality of separation hit her. The unpaved country road was bumpy. So were her feelings. She covered her face with a handkerchief.

The wagon arrived in Masan, and from there she took a passenger ship to Pusan. It was about five in the afternoon when she arrived. Without much thought about leaving the country, she boarded a Japanese steamer bound for Yokohama. It was March, 1918.

Thus, Young Oak became one of almost 1,000 picture brides who left Korea between 1910 and 1924.

Waiting in Yokohama

On the ship, the girl's mind was occupied by imagining her future husband. Memories of her childhood and family in Ham An hardly crossed her mind. Finally the ship crossed the straits separating Korea and Japan. A few days later, the ship reached Yokohama Harbor. At the harbor she was met by her brother and a Korean innkeeper, Mr. Kim Jong Sam. Most of the Korean passengers destined for Hawaii and the American mainland were to stay at Mr. Kim's inn while waiting for the next connection.

The innkeeper handed Young Oak a letter and a check he had received from Mr. Chung Bong Woon. She was surprised by the effective network system of the Korean immigrants. The amount of the check was 200 dollars (400 Japanese yen). In the letter, Mr. Chung instructed his picture bride to take the first-class cabin to make her voyage more comfortable. He warned her about terrible seasickness during the Pacific crossing. Furthermore, he told her that first-class passengers would be exempt from the physical examination. Once again Mr. Chung's thoughtfulness made Young Oak very grateful. She felt already closer to Hawaii than the Ham An she had left a few days before.

She had a different idea for spending the money, however. She decided to take the third-class cabin which would cost only 65 yen. She didn't want to pay a hefty 300 yen for the comfortable first-class cabin. Young Oak gave 300 yen to her student brother, and she was left with only 100 yen. She had not forgotten why she had ventured into the picture marriage in the first place. This was made very clear to Mr. Chung in her numerous letters.

While staying at the Korean inn, she met other picture brides. Some of them were waiting indefinitely for passage fare from their men. She realized for the first time how lucky she was to be matched with someone like Mr. Chung who was willing and able to spend so much. She also found out that some of the so-called picture brides were widows.

A few were with children from their previous marriage. Unlike the virgin picture brides, the widows acted bold and smart.

Occasionally the Korean innkeeper would lend money for the passage fare if some of his guests had to wait too long at Yokohama. At that point, he was more concerned about the picture brides than a possible loss of money. He simply counted on the consciences of the guests he would help. Young Oak was deeply touched by the good deed of the man who helped fellow countrymen in a foreign land.

Like any third-class passenger, Young Oak had to take the physical examination. It mainly consisted of an eye infection check and a stool test. Others told Young Oak that the Yokohama test was more stringent than the one she had in Seoul. This made her nervous.

She passed the eye infection test the first time but failed the stool test. The Japanese doctor told her that she was carried common parasites, and he put her on a heavy dosage of a parasite eradication drug.

From other Koreans staying at the inn, she heard that sometimes it took two or three months to clear parasites. This worried Young Oak a lot. The prospect of waiting so long made her depressed. Now she deeply regretted not taking Mr. Chung's advice to purchase the first-class fare. Moreover, it was too late to change her status.

After carefully thinking over the parasite problem, Young Oak decided to use a trick. She approached another picture bride who passed the physical test quite sometime ago but was still waiting for the fare from her future husband. Young Oak noticed that the lady was very upset about her pitiful situation. She kept blaming herself for having delved into the marriage. The despairing girl told others that she was already experiencing what was in store for her in Hawaii.

Young Oak bought a nice face cream to bribe the lady for a piece of her clean stool. They both knew it was a serious fraud. If such a trick were uncovered, both would be deported to Korea. But the mutual sympathy outweighed the potential risk. It was a friendly deal between two picture brides in a time of difficulty.

Young Oak submitted the other lady's stool in the container clearly marked with her name. A few days later, Young Oak was declared medically clear. She was delighted things were going in her favor. The other girls at the inn envied Young Oak whose future husband was so considerate and rich.

When Young Oak saw a young, happy Korean couple affectionately holding hands, she felt like asking Mr. Chung to come to Yokohama to escort her to Hawaii. She soon realized, however, the time and money Mr. Chung would have to sacrifice just to satisfy her own vanity. If she had known how old he looked, she would not have imagined such a fantasy.

One day she asked other picture brides at the inn what marriage was all about. A 21-year-old bride shared her idea of marriage with Young Oak. "Marriage means that a man and woman sleep together in the same room. As time passes, the wife bears children for her husband and learns to take care of the household chores. That's how you become a wife and mother."

It sounded quite unreal to Young Oak. She could not understand the meaning of sleeping together and bearing children. She wondered how these things happened.

Some long-time Korean residents in Yokohama were visiting the inn to gather up-to-date information about their hometown and the country. Old ladies chided the brides. "I don't understand why you nice-looking girls want to go to Hawaii. Haven't you heard all sorts of miserable stories about picture marriage? Can't you find a decent man in your village? It is never too late to change your mind. Remember it is an unpardonable sin to cause heartache to your old parents and have them miss you until they are buried. Not having seen their loved ones so long, they will never close their eyes when they die."

No bride seemed to pay attention to the typical scoldings they had heard so many times.

Young Oak heard similar advice in Korea, but it sounded more real in Yokohama. However, she felt that her fate was locked with that of Mr. Chung Bong Woon.

While waiting at the inn for the next ship, Young Oak met a Christian lady who was on her way to join her husband in Hawaii. She had worked for years as a housekeeper for an American missionary family in Korea. Her husband had been the caretaker for the same family; that was where they had met. She could converse in English, and she looked quite American. Young Oak envied the sophisticated lady.

She told the brides that only strong faith in God would assure true happiness and prosperity in marriage. She invited everyone to her Bible study from five to six-thirty every morning, but only a few bothered to attend it.

Young Oak was deeply touched by the Bible studies, and she decided to dedicate her life to God. She often wished she could spend the rest of her life just praying and meditating in a remote mountain village. She would have returned to Korea if she had not come this far to marry Mr. Chung in Hawaii.

To avoid the ridicule of other girls who had become cynical and fatalistic, Young Oak used her closet for personal worship. With the closet door open about five inches for light, she read the Bible and prayed. She asked for divine guidance as she continued her journey into the uncertain future.

Young Oak felt really sorry for the Christian lady who had decided to return to Korea. From others the Christian lady had heard that her husband was having an affair with another woman in Hawaii. This shocking news caused her to dedicate her life to church work in Korea rather than to pursue an uncertain married life in Hawaii. Young Oak had mixed feelings about the lady's decision.

Farewell in Yokohama

As Young Oak was preparing for the final leg of the voyage, she had mixed feelings of joy and sadness. Yokohama was a foreign city, yet she could speak Japanese, and she was quite familiar with the Japanese customs. In addition, her brother's frequent visits from Tokyo and her accommodations with a group of Korean guests made her feel at home. And the land of Korea is not that far away. She still had no idea about her final destination except letters from the man with whom she had been corresponding with for months.

The night before her scheduled departure, the innkeeper and the girls got together to give a farewell party for Young Oak. Young Oak bought rice cake (mozzi), sweet candies, and cider. She was in a good mood, but the other girls who were still waiting for passage money or medical clearance were sad about their fate. As the farewell party progressed, the girls began to sing popular Korean folk songs.

Arirang Arirang Arariyo
He is going over the Arirang Hill.
The lover who has left me alone
Will have a sore foot
Before he walks ten ri (three miles).

Arirang Arirang Arariyo
He is going over the Arirang Hill.
There are so many stars in the clear sky,
So many troubles in our lives.

Please look at me
Please look at me
Please look at me
Please look at me as if
You are looking at a flower in December.
Ari Arirang
Sri Srirang

Arariga Natne
Please let me go over
The Arirang Hill.

Although the loved one came from afar
I was too shy to greet him.
I just made a slight smile
While covering my lips with the apron.
Ari Arirang
Sri Srirang
Arariga Natne
Please let me go over
The Arirang Hill.

As they sang the familiar folk songs about love and separation, they all cried. Their hopes and curiosity about the
romantic life in Hawaii were fading quickly. Instead they
were overwhelmed by self-pity and home sickness. Some
cried uncontrollably, calling "Mother," "Father." They
pleaded, "Please take me home. Take me home."

As they regained calm, they wondered why they had
ever wanted to marry someone they had never met and who
lived so far away from Korea.

Encounters in the Immigration Station

Amid huggings, hand-holdings, and farewell wishes,
Young Oak boarded the Japanese-registered ship "Chun
Yang Hwan." Young Oak's brother was deeply emotional as
his little sister embarked on the long journey all alone.
Moreover, he had a painful heartache when he realized that
she had chosen a picture marriage mainly to help him and
the family.

On the ship, there were only three Korean passengers,
the rest were all Japanese. The Chun Yang Hwan left
Yokohama on April 23, 1918.

As the land of Japan slipped below the horizon, Young Oak suddenly felt the pain of separation from loved ones. Although Japan was a foreign country, she at least had a brother there. But now she was bound for a land of strangers. This made her feel much closer to Mr. Chung Bong Woon. Now he was the only person to whom she could turn. She took out his picture and whispered to it, "Master Chung, I am so grateful for your help. I will never forget what you have done for my family."

Many passengers were lying flat, terribly weakened from sea-sickness, but Young Oak did not experience any of that. She enjoyed every moment of the sail. It was fun to watch jumping fish during the day and shimmering stars hanging over the Pacific Ocean during the night. She ate well and slept well. Full of excitement, she walked around the deck singing her favorite songs.

The only unpleasant experience she encountered during the crossing was the death of a Japanese passenger. After a brief ceremony on the deck, the crew threw the body into the sea. The wrapped body quickly sank.

As the days passed, she felt closer to Hawaii. After nine days, the ship finally docked in Honolulu. It was May 1, 1918.

Her first impression of Honolulu from the deck of the ship was somewhat disappointing. The city was not comparable either to Seoul or Yokohama in size and appearance. The drab buildings looked small and scattered.

The immigrants were led to a separate building by officers. The immigration building appeared stark, and the windows were covered with heavy steel bars. Young Oak wondered why the building was made to look like a prison. She was a bit surprised by the meals served there. Almost every meal was a typical Japanese serving: a bowl of rice, miso soup, pickled yellow roots (takuan), and either roasted or fried fish.

As she looked out the window, she saw mostly dark-skinned people (Hawaiians) in the street. Most people waiting in the station seemed to be Japanese. She didn't quite feel that she had come to the fairyland she had dreamed of so long.

Soon she met two Korean picture brides who had left Yokohama a few days before her. Young wondered why they were still in the immigration station. One of the depressed picture brides explained, "We are still waiting for our men. Somehow they cannot leave the sugar plantation. We don't know how we got mixed up in this picture marriage business." They cried.

Young Oak discovered a worse case. The bride had left exactly two ships before Young Oak. By the time Young Oak met her, she had grown disgusted. According to her story, the service refused to admit her into the country because they found she had developed an eye infection during the voyage. The service ordered her to return to Japan for treatment. She would be admitted only after her infection was completely cured. She kept cursing the service for refusing to take care of her eye problem in Honolulu.

Young Oak felt terrible about the predicament of another picture bride, and she could not understand the reason for the ridiculous order. She wondered if Honolulu was so rudimentary in medical care that no one was able to treat the problem.

Unexpectedly Young Oak received a package from Mr. Chung Bong Woon. It was sent in by the Korean innkeeper in Honolulu, Mr. Chung Yoon Phil. In it, she found five large-size oranges and a note by the innkeeper. The note read: "A hearty welcome to Hawaii. Mr. Chung Bong Woon will come to meet you by the first ferry boat leaving Maui Island where he works. Chung Yoon Phil."

She enjoyed the juicy, sweet oranges and was buoyant at the thought of meeting her future husband soon. She also loved the fresh pineapples she bought from a Japanese vendor in the compound of the immigration service. She spent her last seven yen for pineapples. Contrary to first impressions, the taste of Hawaii was pleasant.

On the third day of waiting, a Korean translator by the name of Cho Byung Woo called out Young Oak's name. Then he handed her a package and told her that Mr. Chung Bong Woon had come for an interview with the immigration officer. He told her that she would see Mr. Chung when her own interview was over. The cheerful translator teased Young Oak, "Mr. Chung Bong Woon is a lucky man to marry such a lady who is so cute and well-mannered."

When she realized that her future husband was in the same building and breathing the same air, she felt like jumping up and down like a little child. Her euphoria was indescribable.

Finally, the time of Young Oak's interview came. The translator briefly told her what to expect. He cautioned that he was not supposed to explain the interview procedure. She tried to recall the English words that she had memorized, to sort out the right words for the different phases of the interview.

Then Mr. Cho led Young Oak to an immigration officer. She was nervous, but the presence of the Korean translator helped. She was really glad that she had found a compatriot at a tense moment such as this. When they entered the office, the Korean translator got something from an officer and gave it to Young Oak without saying a word. It was a sheet of paper and pencil. On the paper, a sentence was written both in Korean and English. The written instruction was simple. "Take this paper and pencil to the right side of the immigration officer and give them to the officer with both hands." It was a literary test for the entering foreign immigrants. The Korean translator kept silent while watching Young Oak somewhat nervously.

As instructed on the paper, Young Oak took the paper and pencil to the immigration officer sitting behind a large desk. As she passed cautiously before the officer to reach his right side, Young Oak politely said, "Excuse me," in English. This surprised the immigration officer.

The pleased officer turned to the Korean translator and said, "Mr. Cho, this lady can speak English. She doesn't have to go through all the routines. She passes."

As the translator conveyed the message, Young Oak was delighted about the easy pass, and she felt good about the English lessons she had initiated at home. Later she heard that some illiterate picture brides had been sent home. The immigration service argued that a person illiterate in the mother tongue would be a burden to the United States.

After a while, both Mr. Chung Bong Woon and Lee Young Oak were called in before the officer who tested Young Oak. The two stood side by side, but Young Oak was too shy to look at Mr. Chung.

Through the Korean translator, the immigration officer asked Mr. Chung, "Mr. Chung Bong Woon, is this the woman you have invited to marry?"

"Yes," Mr. Chung replied firmly.

Turning to Young Oak, he asked a similar question through the translator. "Miss Lee Young Oak, is this the man you saw in the picture, and did you come to marry him?"

Young Oak answered without hesitation. "Yes. I came to marry Mr. Chung Bong Woon."

The officer smiled at them. After hastily filling out a form, he turned to the couple. "Congratulations. Now you are ready to go. I wish you a happy married life here in Hawaii."

3

THE WEDDING

The two walked out of the office where they had been interviewed. Mr. Chung led the way and, according to Korean custom, his picture bride followed him about three feet behind. As the two entered the station lobby, they turned around and looked at each other face to face for the first time. Mr. Chung stood about the same height as his bride. As seen in the picture, he had grown a mustache which did not quite match his right angle crew cut. The hem of the old black coat he wore almost touched his knees. Young Oak thought that it might be the style in Hawaii. The outfit made him look clumsy. For a few moments she alternately stared and smiled at him.

"I feel very sorry to make you wait so long for me," Young Oak, bowing politely, finally ventured to speak. "With the money you sent me, I had a pleasant voyage. I am deeply grateful for all the things you have done for me and my family."

Mr. Chung smiled, "I hope you had an enjoyable voyage. Did you get sea-sick?"

"Not at all. I ate and slept well aboard the ship," his bride cheerfully answered.

Mr. Chung gave his right hand to Young Oak to lead her out of the station lobby. Young Oak slightly jerked when she held his hand. She seemed to be holding a palm that was as hard as rock. As he opened the lobby door, half a dozen Koreans waiting outside the immigration building warmly welcomed the couple. The ladies in the welcoming party kindly patted Young Oak on the back.

One of the women said, "Mr. Chung, you are a lucky man to bring such a nice bride from Korea. She must have been born into a good family." Mr. Chung just smiled, not saying much.

They drove an old Ford to a Korean inn located less than a mile from the building. The couple checked into a special corner room the innkeeper had reserved especially for them. Since the innkeeper had the same last name as Mr. Chung, they called each other "brother." Because of this close relationship, the wife of the innkeeper was very kind to Young Oak, as if she were her own sister.

Young Oak began to feel at home in Hawaii. The first meal at the inn reinforced this. On the table she saw nothing but familiar Korean dishes, including kimchi, hot bean paste, (go choo jang), and rice wrapped in lettuce (sam).

Because she craved Korean food after so many days of Japanese food on the ship and at the immigration station, she made and ate half a dozen balls of sam. Each time her cheeks bulged as she tried to chew the oversize rice ball. In amazement, Young Oak asked the wife of the innkeeper if they could buy lettuce here in Hawaii.

"Of course. You can buy literally everything you want. It is like Korea as far as food is concerned," the wife of the innkeeper proudly explained.

The innkeeper's wife was so pleased Mr. Chung Bong Woon had gotten such a cheerful bride. She had seen many Korean picture brides who did nothing but cry day and night from the moment they checked into the inn. Their men went almost crazy not knowing how to handle their strange brides.

Even after the crying phase, some picture brides remained so upset they wouldn't speak a word to anyone for days. They would emerge from the room to eat and then withdraw into the room again. Only the men's threats to deport the girls back to Korea forced them to marry the men they came for. To the wife of the innkeeper, Young Oak seemed an unusually nice bride.

The innkeeper's wife had also heard many heart-breaking stories about picture marriages. As they looked at their future husbands from the deck, their dreams of a new life in Hawaii were shattered for the picture brides. Although they were mentally prepared for a possible disappointment, the men they came to marry looked too old and boorish. The older bachelors who were usually in their 30's and 40's were badly tanned, wrinkled, and even bent from years of hard labor under the sizzling Hawaiian sun. Plantation life without the care of a family made them look much older than their age.

So shocked were some picture brides that they refused to leave the ship and desperately begged the crew to take them back to Korea, but such a plea was ignored. The crew knew that the brides did not have money to pay for return passage. Even if the brides promised to pay the fare upon return, hardly any crew believed their parents' ability to pay, let alone their willingness to take their daughters back. Thus, the brides were forced off the ship by the crew while their men watched helplessly from the pier. Then they would be led into the immigration service building as if they had been taken to a slaughter house. Some turned hysterical and let out the agonizing cry, "Mother, Mother, take me home. Take me home."

After lunch, the innkeeper suggested that Mr. Chung be married that evening. He listed a number of reasons. "Today is Wednesday. If you marry this evening right after the midweek service, that takes care of inviting people.

I can arrange for your wedding with the pastor. Secondly, if you have to wait until Saturday or Sunday, you will have to use two separate rooms until the wedding day. This will double the lodging cost."

Mr. Chung and Young Oak appreciated the practical considerations of the innkeeper. Neither Mr. Chung nor his picture bride raised any objection to the strict Confucian moral code practiced at the inn. So they agreed to marry that evening. The wedding was less than eight hours away. So Mr. Chung asked Young Oak to go shopping for their wedding.

Accompanied by two Korean men who were residents of Honolulu, the two went to the downtown shopping streets. Mr. Chung bought Young Oak a pair of shoes, a gold wedding ring, and a fancy comb studded with colorful corals. Young Oak made sure that the pair of shoes she was trying on would not make her taller than her husband during the wedding ceremony.

The two accompanying bachelors teased Mr. Chung for his willingness to buy anything his bride asked for. They were surprised by the amount of money Mr. Chung was spending without any hesitation. "Mr. Chung, you have worked so hard for so many years on the plantation. What is the money for? Buy anything for your new bride on this once-in-a-lifetime occasion. Isn't money for spending?"

They hurried back to the inn so they would not be late for the wedding.

Wedding and Strange Reception

In their best dress, the couple sat in the front row of the Honolulu Korean Methodist Church. Young Oak was wearing the Chima Jugori her mother made specially for the wedding. There was no pew in the church, and people were sitting on the floor. About 50 people came to attend the midweek service. When the service began, the pastor of the church, Reverend Bang Ha Joong, announced that there would be a brief wedding ceremony immediately afterwards. He made a special appeal to his congregation to stay for the wedding of Mr. Chung Bong Woon and Miss Lee Young Oak.

As soon as the service was over, the pastor asked the two to come forward and stand before him. There was no wedding march, no bridesmaid, and no best man. Yet the pastor seemed to follow all the routine procedures of a typical Christian wedding, including the wedding vow. After the closing prayer, the pastor introduced the newly married couple, Mr. and Mrs. Chung Bong Woon, to his congregation.

Although Young Oak was all alone at her wedding, it did not bother her. She hardly thought about her parents at home. Rather, she was happy and excited about the beginning of a new life in a new country.

As if it were a custom of the church, the pastor asked the couple to march around the congregation for an introduction. The two walked slowly around the people in a circle, Young Oak holding her husband's left arm. The church members clapped for the couple who looked more like father and daughter than husband and wife. But no one seemed to care about the obvious age difference between the groom and the bride. The bride looked slightly taller than the groom. Young Oak heard some people whisper to each other with a surprised look, "Look at the bride. She is smiling and holding her head up. She must be happy."

Young Oak said to herself, "Why shouldn't anyone be happy on one's wedding day?" Only later, she realized the meaning of the comment.

During the circular march, the groom whispered to his bride, "Aren't you shy?" But the bride only smiled without saying a word.

As the two completed the circle, the pastor invited the well-wishers to go to the inn for the wedding reception.

When they got back to the inn, Mr. Chung left his bride alone in the reserved corner room. He asked her to wait there until the party was over. Then he went down-stairs where the wedding reception was about to begin.

Soon Young Oak heard the loud noise of laughter and singing. She wondered if it was the American custom not to let the bride attend the reception. Even in Korea, the reception would be held in the presence of both bride and groom. The brave bride was about to venture into the recep-tion hall, but she restrained herself so as not to offend Mr. Chung. Then all of a sudden, she began to wonder why Mr. Chung's hand was so hard and calloused. She could not figure it out.

About half an hour later, Mr. Chung brought a bowl of ice cream and cookies to his bride and left the room without saying much. Young Oak really liked the sweet ice cream and cookies. She felt like asking for more, but she re-strained herself so as not to show impropriety.

Suddenly, Young Oak felt fatigue overcoming her. It had indeed been a hectic day. So many important things in her life had taken place in such a short time. Going through the tense entry interview at the immigration of-fice, meeting Mr. Chung, shopping, and finally the wed-ding--everything took place within twelve hours. One more ritual of passage in her life awaited her, to face the first night with her husband. But she was too tired to worry about it.

Leaning against the painted oriental folding screen, she fell asleep. It was around midnight when Young Oak woke up at the sound of knocking at the door. She quickly com-posed herself.

"It is me," Mr. Chung informed her.

He grumbled that the guests had just left and seemed a little bit apologetic to his bride. "I am sorry for having left you alone so long. I could not leave the party while the guests were celebrating my own wedding. We are very tired. After changing clothes, let's sleep." He went behind the screen and changed his clothes.

For the first time Young Oak faced a man without street clothing on. At the same time, she realized that she was the only other human being in the room. This made her feel tense, even scared.

Again looking at the bewildered bride, he asked her to change her clothes behind the screen. It was a signal to prepare for the wedding night.

"The touch of my hand may feel hard to you. My palms and fingers are calloused from repeated blisters," the groom cautioned.   Then he jumped on the bed and lay with his right arm under his head, as if he wanted to see every movement of his young bride. Young Oak changed into the night dress her mother specially made for the first night. Young Oak was puzzled because her mother told her that on the first night the groom would be the one to undress the bride.

Coming out from behind the screen, Young Oak didn't know what to do next. As she hesitantly approached the bed, Mr. Chung pulled her hand toward him. At that moment, she began to tremble, not knowing how to react under the circumstances. Out of desperation, she pleaded with him, "Can we marry without touching each other?" Then she dropped on the floor beside the bed. Every time the groom tried to touch her in the dark, she shrank into a crouched position like a shrimp. She cried while trembling like a lost young bird, and the frustrated groom kept puffing a cigar.

She did not understand what the pastor had meant when he said "two bodies become one." No one had given her adequate instruction as to how she should approach the honeymoon night. Again pulling her hand toward him, he said, "Well, this is a part of married life."

The first night was full of fears and tears for the young bride. She hardly slept.

Honeymoon in Honolulu

The next morning Young Oak could not dare to look at her husband. For the first time, she felt an indescribable shame. As she kept her head down, Mr. Chung raised her chin, "Why don't you look at me? Don't be ashamed. We are married now," and then he chuckled.

As they entered the inn's dining room for breakfast, the wife of the innkeeper met them with a big smile. Other guests staying at the inn congratulated the couple. Again the innkeeper's wife began praising Young Oak.

"Mr. Chung is indeed a lucky man. His wife is a rare kind of picture bride. I never take it for granted seeing a newly-wed couple coming to breakfast so happy. I have been in this business long enough to see all sorts of sad things happen to picture marriages. Sometimes I cannot sleep the whole night when I have to mediate between the fighting couples. Usually the disappointed brides would desperately fight back the husbands who try to approach them. Then the women scream as their husbands hit them out of anger and frustration. Sometimes we have to break into the rooms when we think that the couple has become too violent. I think picture marriages have made many young women and old men crazy."

Mr. Chung looked really content and happy with his new wife. His friends suggested that he stay about a week in Honolulu for a honeymoon. They told him that he had worked for 15 years on the plantation without much joy and pleasure. Therefore, he should treat himself as well as his young wife before they went back to the sugar plantation on Maui. They kept telling him that money was for spending, not for saving. The hard-working, thrifty plantation worker accepted the friendly suggestion and decided to take a long honeymoon in Honolulu.

The innkeeper volunteered to drive the couple around in his Ford. Young Oak was pleased to see so many different tropical trees and flowers. For the first time, she tasted wild bananas and other tropical fruits that she picked from the trees. She began to love Hawaii for its weather and beautiful scenery.

The couple grew affectionate. They enjoyed their honeymoon without worrying about Young Oak's parents in

Korea or the harsh life on the sugar plantation. After the ten-day honeymoon, Young Oak felt as if she had lived with her husband for ten years. She respected the man she had married.

During the honeymoon, Young Oak came to know more about her husband's background and personality. Mr. Chung Bong Woon was born in Boryung county in Choong Chung Province on January 1, 1876. He was the only son in his family. The preceding two generations of Chungs also had only one son. This made him a very special figure because the continuity of the family would depend on the only son. He had an older sister who had married a Royal Korean Army general. Perhaps through this connection, he joined the Royal Korean Army. But his army career didn't last long.

Around the time he left the army, the Hawaiian sugar companies widely advertised to recruit Korean workers. In spite of the fact that he was the only son in the family, the desperate, unemployed, former soldier applied for a sugar plantation job in Hawaii.

In 1904, he left Korea only three months after his first marriage. His plan was to return to Korea after saving enough money. But not knowing how long it would take to do so, he just asked his wife to wait until she heard from him. Mr. Chung was sad when he found out that his wife had married another man within a year of his departure. She thought that he had gone too far to return, and Mr. Chung couldn't do anything about his wife's decision back in Korea.

He worked very hard and saved every penny with the intent of returning home. He restrained himself from spending money on items such as clothes and shoes. He told Young Oak that he was still wearing the same clothes he had brought from Korea. He had not bought even a wrist watch, a very popular status symbol among the men.

But as the years went by, he decided not to return to his colonized homeland when Japan finally annexed Korea in 1910. His hatred became very intense. He strongly believed that someday Japan would be defeated. As he decided to settle down in Hawaii, he began looking for a Korean woman. Like many of his fellow Korean workers, he wanted to try picture marriage, and he contacted the marriage broker in Honolulu. When he was shown three pictures and given the first choice as a favor by the broker, he picked the picture of Young Oak.

Mr. Chung Bong Woon, too, came to know more about his wife's family. Young Oak was born on October 25, 1901, in Ham An, Kyung Sang Province. She was the second of the six children and the oldest of the three girls. Her parents were Lee Suk Joon (father) and Hwang Bong Yi (mother).

Her hometown, Ham An, was a small inland town surrounded by mountains. It was the seat of Ham An county. Since Ham An has higher mountains in the south, the Nam Kang river flows to the north. For centuries the people of other towns considered Ham An unfavorable because the reverse flow of the river around Ham An was interpreted as a rebellion against the kings in the capital city.

Young Oak's father was about six feet tall and handsome. Because of his height and fair skin, the people around Ham An suspected that he was of mixed blood. According to one speculation Young Oak heard from others, her paternal grandmother might have been raped by a Russian, which resulted in a shameful pregnancy. As soon as Young Oak's father was born, the child was raised in secret for the first few years. As a merchant, her father traveled to big cities and was well informed of the major events of the world. He loved his first daughter, Young Oak, and he bought rare items such as leather shoes for her.

The newly married couple enjoyed everything Honolulu offered.

4

LIFE ON THE PLANTATION

The sweet honeymoon in Honolulu was soon over. The time came to return to the reality of plantation life. The couple took a small ferry bound for Maui Island. Mr. Chung was sick most of the time, but this time his young wife patiently attended him. He told his wife that he had been terribly sea-sick when he was coming to meet her ten days before. Young Oak could imagine the poor little man suffering all alone without anyone's care. Mr. Chung sincerely thanked her for her comforting words and tender care. After eight hours of sailing, they finally arrived at the Kahului port and took a taxi to the plantation.

The Koreans on the plantation were surprised to see Mr. Chung accompanied by a young, cheerful woman. One of them bluntly told Mr. Chung, "Since you took so long, we thought that you had deported your picture bride for refusing to marry you. Otherwise you would not have stayed so many days in Honolulu. At least you should have informed us that you would stay longer in Honolulu for the honeymoon. All along we have been really worried about you. Anyhow, we are extremely happy to see you with your bride." Then they told the couple that there would be a reception that evening at the Korean Methodist Church.

No one dared to imagine that the thrifty old bachelor would take a ten-day honeymoon in the big city. Skipping so many work days and spending so much money in Honolulu was completely uncharacteristic of the Mr. Chung they had known.

The company house waiting for the newly married couple was a small but neat dwelling about a hundred feet away from the neighbors' houses. The house had a living room, a bedroom, and a small storage space with the toilet and kitchen detached. The roofed kitchen had a dining table beside an open fireplace for cooking. Cooking was done by firewood. In the bedroom, Young Oak saw a double-bed with a mosquito net drawn over it and a shiny Singer sewing machine along side. Young Oak loved the brand-new mosquito net, a luxury item in Korea. Here and there, she also noticed gas lamps and candles for lighting. (Electricity would not be brought to the plantation for another year.)

"This is a nice new house," the young wife exclaimed with pleasure.

"Yes, a newly married wife deserves a nice new house," Mr. Chung piped in delightedly.

He took his wife around the house, giving brief instructions. He also showed where food was stored and how to use the outdoor kitchen. Everything was neatly arranged. He said he would start working the next day and that breakfast should be ready no later than 4:30 in the morning.

In the evening they went to the Korean Methodist Church. All six Korean workers and their families living on the plantation compound gathered in the church. Some bachelor workers also came to the reception. About ten families living on other plantations around could not come because of distance. The workers and their families dressed properly for the occasion—celebrating the marriage of their community head (dong jang). The deputy head formally welcomed the couple, and Mr. Chung politely thanked him and his fellow workers for the hearty welcome.

While serving cookies and cider, the workers asked Young Oak to tell them about the situation at home, especially the relationship between Koreans and Japanese. Young Oak didn't hesitate.

"I may compare the relationship between the Koreans and Japanese to that of fire and water. The two peoples don't get along with each other at all. So many times I have seen Japanese sanitation workers slapping and kicking Korean women for not complying with sanitation orders, such as hanging clothes in the sun at least once a month. I have heard that they try to dye the white clothes of Koreans with black ink to dampen the spirit of the Korean people. Whenever Japanese constables come to settle a dispute between Koreans, they swear at both parties and sometimes they beat both indiscriminately. Korean Christians are restricted in their worship service and other religious activities. Japanese demand that Koreans worship their Emperor. Gradually they take over the choice farm lands and houses. Sighs of Koreans reach heaven, and the weight of their groaning shakes the land. Many Koreans at home gnash their teeth over Japanese rule." Then she added, "Please give up the idea of going back to Korea to live. You may not be able to stand the oppression. Settle down in Hawaii and make it your home until our motherland regains independence."

The Korean residents were upset to hear about the worsening political situation back home. Some began to curse the Japanese. Young Oak felt awkward that the wedding reception had turned into a political rally.

To change the mood, a group of women sang a song for the newly married couple. Young Oak responded by singing a song popular in Korea at that time entitled "Thinking of Homeland."

"So many years I have been away from home
The hardship I suffered appears like a mountain
The tears I have shed form a long river
Ah, ah, when can I return to my dear home."

By the time Young Oak had finished the eighth stanza, everyone in the reception was crying, including the singer. She couldn't have picked a worse report of their homeland and a worse song for the sojourners. The Koreans on the sugar plantation, both married and unmarried, were people suffering from terrible homesickness and political frustration. They considered themselves wanderers in a foreign country who had lost their sovereignty to Japan.

Young Oak sincerely apologized for causing sadness on the happy occasion. But the guests told her that they felt good after crying so hard. "You know, crying makes us feel liberated from the Japanese. This is a chance to vent our despair."

On the way home, Mr. Chung firmly ordered his wife not to speak Japanese anywhere, even to the Japanese. He said he might send her back if she should speak Japanese.

Learning of Homemaking

Young Oak could not fall asleep. She was nervous about cooking her first breakfast for her husband because she had not learned much about cooking at home. It was about 2:00 when she got up quietly to cook. When she slipped out to the outdoor kitchen, it was still dark. In the clear sky, stars were shimmering. Not knowing the proper ratio of rice and water, she poured too much rice into the cooking pot. As the rice cooked, she could smell it burning, so she kept pouring water to cool the pot.

At the sound of the alarm clock under the bed, Mr. Chung got up exactly at 4:00. He looked for his wife. When he could not find her anywhere in the house, he instantly thought that she had run away. Only after he found her cooking in the outdoor kitchen, he was relieved.

"What time did you get up?" the husband asked.

"I hardly slept. I didn't want to be late in preparing your breakfast."

Mr. Chung told his wife to use the alarm clock next time. Without a word of complaining about the badly burned rice, he finished the meal and left for the plantation at 4:30. He said he would come home around 5:00 in the afternoon.

In the morning hours Young Oak cleaned the house, but there was not much to do. She waited for her husband the whole afternoon. As soon as she saw him coming home she ran to him, like a little girl awaiting her father's return from a long trip. Taking his lunch pail, she walked happily next to him. He looked extremely tired, and his trousers were covered with wet red mud up to the waist line.

"So how did you spend the day at home? Weren't you bored? There is not much to do here in the plantation. People hardly visit each other during the day. Both men and women are too busy making a living," Mr. Chung explained.

After supper, Mr. Chung went straight to bed and fell asleep in a few seconds. Young Oak didn't know that would become the daily routine on the plantation for many years to come.

Young Oak had no luck figuring out the proper ratio of rice and water for cooking. Furthermore, she didn't know that controlling the heat of the fire was the key. She kept burning the rice. In the course of the 30 minutes it takes to cook the rice, she opened the lid about a dozen times to check it. As a result, she usually cooked a three-layer rice: badly burned at the bottom, sticky but cooked in the middle, and raw at the top. One day Mr. Chung complained about eating burned rice day in and day out. He was angry at his wife for serving improperly cooked food. In the old days, burning rice was as serious an offense as infertility. A husband could send his wife away for repeatedly burning it.

For the first time, Young Oak discovered that he had a short temper. He could be nasty if things went bad.

Following his suggestion, she asked other Korean ladies on the plantation about the proper way to cook rice. She realized that she had been using the wrong method in two ways. First, she put in too much rice for the size of the pot. Secondly, it was a mistake to maintain the same heat throughout the cooking. The ladies told her that the secret was the gradual reduction of fire under the pot as the rice simmered. Young Oak regretted that she had not learned the basics of cooking at home.

One day, Mr. Chung asked his wife for clean work clothes. Young Oak told him that she had piled the soiled work clothes in the backyard. She never thought of re-using the heavily soiled work clothes because when dried they weighed about three pounds each and they were as stiff as raw leather. Her irate husband shouted at her, "Are you stupid? How can any man afford throwing away work clothes after just one wearing? I wonder about the state of your mind. I must have brought an immature child, not a mature woman." He kept shaking his head in disbelief.

Young Oak, embarrassed about her ignorance, began to cry. Self-pity overwhelmed the young wife.

"Don't cry," Mr. Chung comforted her. "Learning these things takes time and experience." Then he suggested, "Please go to the Japanese woman next door and see how the washing of soiled work clothes is done."

Young Oak became concerned that Mr. Chung might easily lose his temper again. She followed his suggestion and went to the Japanese neighbor woman to learn about washing. The woman kindly demonstrated how to remove the clay from the cloth and how to starch it. The washing seemed strenuous.

Young Oak repeated the same procedure, but the result was not satisfactory. The wet work clothes hanging on the line still dripped reddish water, not clear water. Later the Korean ladies on the plantation told her to beat the cloth with a hard washing bat to remove the clay.

Not long after the incidents of rice burning and soiled clothes, she heard from other Korean ladies that Mr. Chung might consider sending the teen bride back home. He complained to his fellow workers that his young wife didn't know how to cook and wash. Moreover, he felt pity for his 16-year-old wife struggling all alone far away from home.

He said that some nights she would search about his chest in her sleep, calling out, "Mother, Mother, give me water". He felt terribly guilty living with such a young wife. Of course, he never forgot the first night when his bride was trembling like a baby.

The sympathetic Korean ladies alerted Young Oak. They told her to be careful not to repeat the same mistakes. They also advised Young Oak to act like an adult, even in bed. But Young Oak wondered how she could control talking in her sleep.

This report scared Young Oak. If she was sent back home, not only would this bring shame to her and her entire family but also it would greatly reduce her chances of remarrying a decent man. More important than such personal reasons would be the discontinuance of the financial support from Mr. Chung. She felt that her brothers would need Mr. Chung's help to finish their education in Japan.

One evening after supper, she said to her husband, "Father, I am quick to learn new things. Please teach me and show me how to do things right. I know my lack of experience in life has caused much inconvenience and trouble to you."

Moved by the sincere attitude of his wife, Mr. Chung confessed, "I don't know much about housekeeping either. As you know I have lived alone for almost 20 years in Hawaii. I will teach you the things I am familiar with. You must remember that I am an impatient man. Therefore, I want you to be quick and alert." He also kindly suggested that Young Oak ask other women if she had questions about things of which she was not sure.

She began learning to cook different Korean foods by asking for recipes and cooking methods whenever she was invited to other Korean families. She would try the same dish at her own kitchen following the instruction of her hostess until the taste of her dish turned out about the same as the dish she had tasted.

Lopsided Marital Relation

From the moment Young Oak met Mr. Chung, she never called him "yeubo" (dear, honey), a common, affectionate expression between spouses. She always called him "abuji" (father), even before a baby was born. (Calling one's husband "my children's father" is quite common among Korean wives when children are born. Also men use a similar expression in calling their wives "my children's mother.") She was more comfortable calling him "father" than "dear" or "honey." As a matter of fact, she never considered him a dear, sweet husband.

Moreover, around the plantation she noticed that some Japanese wives called their husbands "odosan" (father). She thought that a wife should call her husband "father" in America. The strict, old-fashioned Mr. Chung considered a woman calling one's husband "yeubo" quite improper. He said only a harlot would use such a vulgar term to her husband. Not knowing the proper American custom for addressing her husband, she didn't feel awkward at all calling him "father."

And she meant what she called him. The relationship between the two was always that of father and daughter rather than that of husband and wife. Young Oak considered Mr. Chung a benevolent father who had saved her family in a time of financial hardship. On top of this, they were a generation apart in age. Mr. Chung's formative years belonged to the 19th century and his wife's to the 20th.

Young Oak's attitude was reciprocated by Mr. Chung who called his wife "child." Affectionate expression was a rare occurrence in the young wife. But neither of them questioned the propriety of the deferential relationship.

Mr Chung also meant what he called her. To the 42-year-old man, the 16-year-old wife was hardly an equal. This was reinforced by his young wife's absolute obedience and respect.

One day, not long after the wedding, Mr. Chung gave his wife a simple English lesson. "If I call you 'you,' know that it is equivalent to 'yeubo' in Korean. In Hawaii that's what we call each other." Young Oak pretended that she didn't know the real meaning of "you". She didn't want to hurt her husband's pride.

Mr. Chung taught his wife some basic American manners. "When you eat soup, you are not supposed to make a noise. It is also the habit of white people not to open the mouth with food in it. Chew your food with lips closed."

Almost every night, Young Oak felt like crying. The loneliness and homesickness was unbearable. Yet she could not cry. Her crying would be understood as a lack of love by her husband. So she cried alone during the daytime. She told herself that she would never let her own children marry someone too faraway and at too young an age.

Bachelor Workers

From time to time, Mr. Chung cautioned his young wife about the temptations of the bachelor workers on the plantation. He firmly ordered her to keep the doors locked during the day time and advised his wife not to walk alone around the plantation while he was at work. "Many Korean families have been ruined by bachelor workers. These men are fond of seducing married women. They are usually lazy, constantly skipping work, using all kinds of sickness including homesickness and woman-sickness, as an excuse. They barely feed themselves. Without money, they cannot afford to bring a picture bride from Korea. Their faces look fair and their hands are soft. While married men are at work, they prey on the naive wives whose husbands are rough and dark from back breaking work in the sugar fields. Foolish wives can not resist the smooth talk and good looks of some former civil servants and scholars."

"Don't worry, father. I will heed your warning."

One morning there was an unexpected knock at the door. When Young Oak opened the door, a Korean man was standing there holding something in his right hand. It was Mr. Lee whom Young Oak had met at the Korean church. The short man in his 40's was a bachelor. "I am sorry for bothering you so early in the day, but I am too sick to go to work. Since I stayed in bed past meal time, I missed breakfast in the cafeteria. Would you mind cooking this ham and making a cup of coffee for me, please?"

Then he handed the bag to Young Oak. She had no choice but to accept the request of the unexpected visitor.

Remembering her husband's frequent warning, Young Oak made the man stay away while she was cooking the ham in the kitchen. As she served the cooked ham, the man invited her to join him, "Thank you, but I had breakfast with my husband before he went to work. You just go ahead."

Then she went back to her room and locked the door. After finishing the food, the displeased and disappointed man left without saying a word to Young Oak. That evening Mr. Chung was very pleased when his wife told him how she handled the unexpected visit by Mr. Lee.

"Father, did I act properly?" Young Oak wanted to hear a compliment from her husband. Also Young Oak knew that if Mr. Chung heard of Mr. Lee's visit it would raise suspicion.

"Yes, you handled yourself well. If you had entertained him by chatting with him, that might have pleased the man for a while. But that could have caused him to desire more visits while I am at work. Remember that there is no tree that can stand continuous chopping. If he comes again for any reason, ask him if it is proper to visit you while I am at work."

After that chilly treatment, Mr. Lee avoided Young Oak. Later at church Young Oak happened to see some Korean bachelors busy staring at women through their loose fingers which covered their faces while others were praying. She saw the seriousness of her husband's warning.

Plantation Life

One day Young Oak noticed a big round scar on her husband's abdomen. She asked what had caused it.

"For years, my job was to irrigate the sugar field," he explained. "It was indeed hard work. Often I had to work for hours in cold water reaching up to my waist. That irrigation job caused severe pains. I often had terrible, terrible pains. After all sorts of Western treatment and medicine, which did not cure the stomach pain, I went to a Korean herb doctor. He applied a tiny ball of herb fire a few times to my stomach. I was really scared to death but that took care of the pain. According to the herb doctor, the vacuum created in the earthen cup by the burning fire sucks the cold out of the stomach. I didn't understand it, but I believed the effects of the treatment."

On a typical day Young Oak's husband worked from 6:00 in the morning until 4:30 in the afternoon, and he worked seven days a week with few exceptions. The daily wage in the earlier years was 69 cents. When he reported to the work stations, he would be assigned to a gang of 20 to 25 men, a mixture of Koreans, Japanese, Chinese, and Filipinos.

Each day's work was determined by the needs of growing sugar plants: planting, weeding, fertilizing, irrigation, and harvesting. The hardest work, however, was weeding and cutting the cane. Ten hours of continuous hoeing under the burning sun made many cry. The workers were under the constant supervision of the luna (field supervisor) who always watched the movement of each. If he spotted any irregularity, such as standing straight to ease the pain, he would shout at or whip the deviant one. During work, chatting with others was prohibited, and the workers had only a 30-minute break for lunch and rest. So when they went home, they barely managed to finish supper and went to bed without delay. Many wives of plantation workers were so discontent with the little time shared with their husbands that they became prey to temptation.

Cutting the sugar cane was really demanding work. Before cutting, the workers burned the dry leaves in order to save just the stems. This produced an excessive amount of ash. For this reason, the field workers looked like ghosts during the harvest. Only their eyes and teeth showed their original color, and the rest of the face was covered with grey ash.

With a heavy machete as long as 20 inches, the workers cut off the dusty canes which were twice as tall as they. Continuous cutting caused multiple blisterings, thus eventually forming thick, calloused palms. Mr. Chung had already worked for 15 years in the sugar field when he brought his wife. Years of hard work had conditioned him into a tenacious, diligent man.

Plantation owners used incentives at different levels to increase worker productivity. To anyone who worked at least 20 days a month, the company would pay a monthly bonus of 5 dollars. The montly bonus was 9 dollars if a worker worked 30 days. Thus, a typical worker putting in at least 20 days a month could earn about 20 dollars a month (14 dollars of regular wage plus the 5 dollar bonus). Hard workers such as Mr. Chung earned about 30 dollars a month (21 dollars of the regular wage and a 9 dollar bonus). In addition, the company would pay end-of-year bonus. Usually, the yearly bonus ranged from 200 dollars to 500 dollars, depending on the annual profit. But one year Mr.

Chung received as much as 1500 dollars for an annual bonus.

A bachelor worker would pay 10 dollars in a month for boarding (three meals a day) and 2 dollars a month for laundry. Before marrying, Mr. Chung could save more than 500 dollars a year.

From the beginning, the Korean workers formed a village council (Dong Hoi) on each plantation. The council was a self-governing organization to maintain order among workers. If someone engaged in deviant behavior, such as excessive drinking, gambling, and fighting, the council members would punish the violator. Korean workers were sensitive not to tarnish the reputation of their country.

Even on the rare Sundays when Mr. Chung was off work, he would get up around 5:00 and work in the vegetable garden around the house. One day Young Oak asked him why he had to get up so early even on his off days. "Father, don't you deserve to relax at least when you are off?"

Young Oak never forgot her husband's answer. "If I stay in bed late on Sundays, other people might think that I indulge too much in my young wife."

Young Oak asked herself what was wrong with that. On the plantation, Young Oak always wished to stay late in bed and sleep as much as she wanted.

Growing Families

One day, Mr. Chung brought fabrics of different color and design. "Since there is not much to occupy your time and mind, make clothes using these fabrics." Then he arranged for the Korean Singer salesman to teach Young Oak how to use the sewing machine. He made sure that the man would come at evenings when he was home.

Not having a pattern to go by, Young Oak ripped apart one of the Chima Jugori she had brought from Korea. Then she drew each piece on paper for a pattern. The idea worked. She used the same method for her children's clothes.

Young Oak also sent some fabric to her mother with her husband's permission. She remembered the mother of Koo who had become the object of envy for her colorful dress. The picture-bride daughter sent home a lot of good quality fabrics.

The only recreation during the week was playing different ball games with other Korean women on the plantation. Usually this took place on Wednesday afternoons when their Westernized pastor, Reverend Hong Anshik, came for the midweek service. Being aware of the monotony of plantation life, the young pastor organized games for women. They really enjoyed a few hours free from their daily routines and mundane concerns. The game always ended before the men came home from the field because they went without the knowledge of the husbands. None of the women wanted to raise suspicion or anger by telling their husbands about this leisurely activity with the pastor.

About six months after the wedding, Young Oak became sick. She felt terribly weak and lost her appetite. Mr. Chung took her to a herb doctor, but his medicine didn't help at all.

Mr. Chung was so worried that he discussed his wife's problem with his fellow workers. One afternoon, an old Korean lady visited Young Oak and inquired about her period. When Young Oak told her that she had skipped a few times, the old lady told her that she was pregnant. This news made the old husband extremely happy, and he treated his pregnant wife with care.

Young Oak was not excited by the news, however. Since she did not consider herself an adult yet, she felt sad and ashamed to be pregnant. She was only 16, and she felt that she had been deprived of childhood forever. Young Oak had barely managed to learn cooking, washing, and sewing. She was not ready to be a mother.

Young Oak gave birth to a healthy boy on June 9, 1919. The couple gave him both Korean and American names: Choonja (child of Spring) and Harry. After Harry was born, she gave birth to a boy every other year until October

8, 1930, when her sixth son was born. At the birth of their last child, Young Oak was 29 years old and her husband 53. Being the only son in the family, Mr. Chung couldn't have been happier with six sons in a row: Harry, William, Walter, Robert, Richard, and Ronald. The spell of having only one son in the Chungs for three consecutive generations finally ended. He was grateful to his young wife for literally multiplying him six times in a matter of ten years. No longer did he have to worry about the discontinuity of his family line. His affection toward his wife grew as the precious sons grew healthy under the care of their loving mother.

Young Oak also grew one inch taller after she came to Hawaii. At the time of entry, her height measured five feet one-and-a-half inches.

Not long after the birth of Ronald, Mr. Chung had a serious accident while working under a plantation locomotive engine. That accident rendered him permanently impotent. He was very upset and depressed about the loss of his procreative power. Without understanding the concept of birth control, the couple might have had even more children. Even so, they would have preferred a large family.

Although Young Oak was disturbed by her husband's accident, she felt relief in not having to worry about going through another pregnancy. At that time, the young wife didn't fully understand how much the accident would affect their marital relation.

The father was strict with his boys. As a former soldier, he was a firm believer in discipline and raised his six boys with unbending rules. For instance, any boy who was late to the table after the father rang the bell would lose his dinner. He was especially hard on his first son, Harry, believing that the example would be critically important to other boys. He would punish Harry for the wrongs of the other boys, blaming him for not supervising the younger brothers properly. He often quoted the Korean saying, "Only when the upper stream is clear, can we expect the down stream to be clear."

Young Oak taught her children absolute obedience to their father. This worked because she herself exemplified unconditional submission to her husband. Whenever the boys were scolded by their father, they would say consistently, "Father, I won't make the same mistake again." Then the father would say, "You must have been coached by your mother." Young Oak would do anything to maintain peace in the family.

The couple believed that nothing should get in the way of their children's education. The father would spend any sum to buy things for the boys' studies. His wife poured all her energy and time into child rearing. She was determined to educate her children so that none of them would have to repeat the lot of their father.

Mr. and Mrs. Chung with their first son, Harry, in 1919 (above)
and with their six sons in 1942 (below)

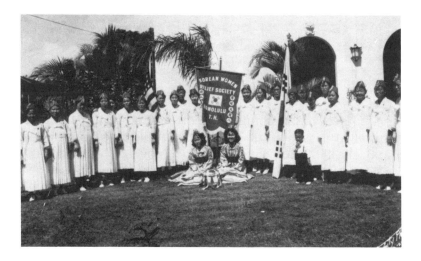

The new picture bride welcomed by Korean and American ladies
(above) and Mrs. Chung with members of the
Korean Women's Relief Society

⑤

THE DISTURBED
COUNTRY OF
MORNING CALM[1]

Undoubtedly, the coming of Mr. Chung Bong Woon to Hawaii as well as that of his picture bride was a matter of personal choice. But their personal decisions were not divorced from the effects of many political events in Korea and neighboring nations.

From the time of Mr. Chung's birth in 1876 to the time of his picture bride's departure in 1918, a span of a little over 40 years, Korea had gone through turbulent political condition at the hands of foreign powers. During this period, the faltering Yi Dynasty was caught in the middle of many cross winds blowing from various directions. Eventually, the dynasty succumbed to external forces and an end came to its 500-year reign in 1910. Thus the Yi dynasty, characterized as a "hermit kingdom" or a country of "morning calm," became a chapter in the history of Korea.

In the midst of the turmoil the two commoners in our story, who were almost a generation apart, came to Hawaii in search of a better life. They did not see much hope for their own future in Korea. Yet they didn't forget their country. Even after they settled in Hawaii, they continued to support Korea in her struggle to regain independence. What makes the story of this couple significant is the interweaving of their histories with the modern history of their country. The interweaving did not take place accidentally but by conscious effort. Therefore, the modern history of Korea, spanning the combined lifetimes of the two, is presented here as background to their biographies.

For centuries, Korea was the object of keen interest to neighbor countries. The country, less than 100,000 square miles, is surrounded by China, Japan, and Russia. Korea shares its northern border with China and Russia along the Yalu and Dumen rivers, which serve as a physical boundary. To the south, Korea and Japan are separated by the narrow Korean straits. On a clear day, people on the south coast of Korea can see the tip of Simonoseki.

In vying for predominance in the Far East, both China and Japan were interested in controlling Korea because of its strategic importance. China needed Korea as an outpost to block any Japanese military move. But her interest in Korea was more than political strategy. Much in Korean culture stemmed from China, and the two countries shared much, including religion, family structure, and literature. Communication was facilitated by their common use of Chinese characters. For centuries, the small peninsular country was content with the status of being a tributary of China.

To the island nation, Japan, the Korean peninsula was an invaluable land bridge, connecting it to the vast Asian continent. Although Japan owed much of its cultural heritage to Korea, gratitude was not expressed. Instead, she tried to conquer her neighbor whenever possible. The first invasion took place in April, 1592, and the invading Japanese army of 150,000, equipped with the newly imported rifle, swept the southern part of Korea. But the Korean army managed to resist.

During the invasion, Admiral Lee Soon Shin invented the world's first ironclad warship, which was shaped like a tortoise. This turned out to be far more devastating to the Japanese than their rifle to the defending Korean army. After seven bloody years of war, Japan gave up her ambition and retreated. The invasion left an unforgettable hatred for the Japanese in the minds of Koreans.

The triangular relationship among the three countries continued until the second half of the 19th century when Western countries began to appear on the scene. They demanded open trade and the establishment of diplomatic relations with Asian countries. This compounded the domestic political situation of Korea.

The powerless hermit kingdom responded to the demand of the West with self-imposed isolation. Apprehensively Korea drew a thick bamboo curtain around herself, and the infamous gunboat diplomacy began along the coast.

In September 1875, the Japanese gunboat Unyoko, while surveying the western coast, was attacked by the Korean army stationed on Kangwha Island. The provocation didn't go unpunished, and the Japanese naval force decisively retaliated.

This incident was followed, through the mediaton of China, by the signing of the Korean-Japanese Treaty on February 26, 1876. (Mr. Chung Bong Woon was born on January 1, 1876.) The treaty seemed an ominous prelude to many Koreans. Among other conditions, it stipulated the establishment of diplomatic relations and the opening of Korean seaports to the Japanese.

The thick veil of isolation was slowly being lifted. This made Korea far more vulnerable to prowling foreign countries.

But China, the long-time guardian country, viewed the treaty between Korea and Japan as the beginning of Japan's influence in Korea and an eventual threat to the security of China. To countervail the increasing Japanese influence, China persuaded the Korean government to establish diplomatic relations with Western powers, especially the United States, which seemed to have no territorial desire over Korea.

The first American attempt to make contact with Korea took place much earlier, however. In May, 1871, the American ship "General Sherman" was cruising the Daedong River in the northwestern region of Korea. To the surprise of the American crew, the Korean army attacked the American ship, and the captain had no choice but to retreat without retaliation.

A few years later, encouraged by the Korean-Japanese Treaty of 1876, the United States government dispatched Commodore Robert W. Shufeldt aboard the U.S.S. Ticonderoga. Through the mediating help of China, a formal treaty was signed between Korea and America on May 22, 1882.[2]

This was the same method the American government had used to open up Japan about 20 years earlier. In the summer of 1853, Commodore Mathew Calbraith Perry had sailed to Tokyo Bay, twice demanding that Japan establish trading relations with the United States. Powerless in defending herself, Japan signed the Treaty of Kanagawa on March 31, 1854.[3]

But Americans were not the first Westerners the Koreans ever encountered. As early as 1653, 36 Dutch sailors drifted to Cheju Island in the South Korean Sea when their merchant ship was wrecked. Hamel, one of eight Dutch sailors who managed to escape from Korea, introduced the hermit kingdom to the West through his book. Thereafter, Korea was occasionally visited by European merchants and missionaries until their countries formally demanded trade and diplomatic relations.

The continual confrontation of China and Japan over the control of Korea led to the Sino-Japanese War. It lasted less than a year from August 1894 to April 1895. The war ended with a Japanese victory, and this ended China's dominance over Korea.

During the post-war settlement, Japan yielded to the pressure of Russia, France, and Germany to give up the Liaotong peninsula, a bounty of the Sino-Japanese War. This concession was interpreted by the Korean government as a weakening of Japan. The precarious, opportunistic Korean government turned to Russia for protection.

This gave Russia hope of obtaining the ice-free, year-round sea ports of Korea. The Russians wanted to link their major east Russian harbor, Vladivostok, to Port Arthur in China. Russia grabbed the opportunity without any hesitation, and it began to exert its influence over the Korean court.

This made Japan fearful of the eastward expansion of Russia, and it intended to block the move. After careful study and preparation, Japan declared war on February 10, 1904. The Russo-Japanese war lasted until September 5 of the following year. During the war Great Britain and the United States supported Japan to keep Russia from dominance in the Far East. Japan emerged from the war as a victor. The two countries signed the Treaty of Portsmouth, which recognized Japan's interests in Korea.

By defeating Korea's two northern neighbors one after the other, Japan had removed the major obstacles to annexation of Korea. In 1910, Japan finished the colonization of Korea, thus ending the last Korean dynasty. In the long 4300-year Korean history, Japan was the first to take away Korean sovereignty.

During these conflicts the Korean people became frustrated and confused. The colonization of Korea by Japan led many Koreans to despair and anger. In spite of their staunch attachment to the village where their parents and ancestors were buried, many chose to leave the homeland. Large numbers went to northern China (Manchuria) and some went to Japan. But Hawaii was not an attractive choice to the Koreans because of its distance and its unfamiliar culture and geography.

Korean Immigration to Hawaii

In the meantime, the expanding sugar industry in Hawaii was experiencing a chronic shortage of workers. To solve the labor problem, the sugar companies first turned to China. However, most Chinese workers would stay only the three contract years and leave the plantation in search of city jobs, primarily in Honolulu. At the same time, the Caucasian plantation owners seriously considered the annexation of Hawaii to the United States as a means of expanding their sugar market. As annexation became more real, they could not overlook the worsening anti-Chinese feeling on the mainland, which resulted in the passage of the Chinese Exclusion Act in 1882.[4]

The Chinese Exclusion Act forced the plantation owners to look for alternative labor sources in the Orient, and Japan was their next choice. However, it did not take long to discover that the Japanese didn't come without trouble. They didn't adjust well to the severe working conditions of sugar plantations. The better-educated, independent-minded Japanese proved less subordinate. Some left the plantation even before the expiration of the contract. Also there were rumors that Japan might attempt to annex Hawaii by promoting the immigration of its people to the islands.[5]

When the Hawaiian Islands finally became a territory of the United States in 1900, a large number of Chinese and Japanese workers moved to the mainland. This left the sugar industry a much smaller pool of workers. So Korea was seriously looked upon as the next source of labor.

The plantation owners then managed to contact the U.S. Minister to Korea, Horace Allen, who was visiting the States at the time. Mr. Allen regarded the Koreans as hard-working and quick-minded. He also thought that the distressing political and economic conditions of the country would motivate many Koreans to go overseas.[6]

Upon returning to Korea, Mr. Allen contracted with David W. Deshler, who was from Ohio like himself. Deshler was conducting a variety of businesses in the Orient, including the operation of a steamship service between Korea and Japan. Deshler quickly realized that he might benefit in transporting Korean laborers. When the preliminary work was done, the Hawaiian Sugar Plantation Association (HSPA) made an offer of 55 dollars to Deshler for every Korean worker he could recruit.[7]

Since Korea signed the Treaty of Trade with the United States in 1882, the diplomatic preparation for such a transaction had been done years before.

The American Minister to Korea easily convinced the Korean king, Emperor Kojong, of the potential benefits if his subjects emigrated to Hawaii. Mr. Allen was a close associate of the king who would lend an attentive ear to the advice offered by the American ambassador on various matters.

The Emperor saw the emigration of his subjects as a bridge between Korea and America. He hoped that such a connection might cause the United States to get involved in the internal affairs of Korea to countervail the increasing influence of Japan on his kingdom.

In 1902, for the first time in the history of Korea, the Korean government set up the Bureau of Emigration to handle emigrants to Hawaii.

Encouraged by the move of the Korean government, David Deshler established the Korean Development Company to manage advertisement and recruitment. The smart businessman also set up Deshler Bank to loan passage and "show money" to the applicants. The Korean Development Company advertised for labor in the major port cities, such as Inchon, Pusan, and Wonsan.

The advertisement said that each worker would work 10 hours a day, six days a week, and earn 16 dollars a month (65 cents a day). It said that the sugar company would provide free housing, fuel, water, education for children, and medical care. The only things the workers might have to buy would be food, clothes, and personal items.[8]

Contrary to the high hopes of the emigration promoters, the response was unexpectedly low. The disappointed American Ambassador, Horace Allen, turned to the Protestant missionaries to help recruit as many Korean workers as possible. He knew it would work, because the American missionaries were sympathetic with the political struggle of their host country and enjoyed the trust of the people. Moreover, enlightened Koreans considered the American missionaries a symbol of modernization.9

Of special interest was Reverend George Herber Jones. He became so enthusiastic in promoting the Hawaiian emigration that he succeeded in persuading nearly half of his Inchon Yongdong congregation to emigrate.

In spite of the age-old Korean norm that an honorable man would not leave his parents and the graves of his ancestors, the wedge of the promotion campaign slowly made cracks on hard-rock tradition. Furthermore, many sensed that their hermit kingdom was nearing its end thanks to the encroachment of Imperial Japan. On top of continual political predicaments, the country suffered severely from years of widespread drought and famine. People in the lower class especially were desperate for survival.10

On December 22, 1902, the first shipload of 121 left Inchon Harbor aboard the "S. S. Gaelic" for Kobe, Japan. At Kobe, 19 failed the physical examination. Thereafter, the S. S. Gaelic continued to sail toward its destination with 102. The first group included 56 men, 21 women, and 25 children. They arrived in Honolulu on January 13, 1903.11 About two years later, in November 1904, Mr. Chung Bong Woon came.

During the first wave of Korean emigration between 1903 and 1905, a total of 7,226 Koreans came to Hawaii aboard 65 ships. They were 6,048 men, 637 women, and 541 children.12 The Korean emmigrants were drawn from all walks of life—former soldiers, house servants, miners, woodcutters, and unskilled laborers. More than half were illiterate.

Even before the arrival of Koreans in Honolulu, the plantation operators divided the incoming workers among themselves. Upon the completion of entry procedures, they transported the workers to assigned plantations scattered on the various islands. They used small boats or wagons to distribute the new arrivals.

Married workers were given a small, two-room house, and the bachelors were kept in large barracks. Bachelor workers were grouped according to nationalities. They slept in bunker beds and ate in the big kitchen.

Some plantations were run like military camps. For instance, camp residents were expected to be in bed by 8:30 after which no light was allowed. They got up at 5:00 in the morning by the camp whistle. To make sure that everyone was ready for work, camp policemen would go through the camps shouting "get up, get up." If some were slow, the policemen would kick in the door, then whip and chase the workers out of bed. After breakfast, they gathered on the plantation yard, and work groups were led by field foremen to assigned tasks for the day. Such a regimented routine was repeated day in and day out.13

After three years of continuous influx, the wave of Korean emigration came to a sudden halt in 1905, to the great disappointment of the plantation owners. Two incidents were attributed to the ending of the Korean immigration in Hawaii.

First about 1,000 Koreans were misled by a British recruiter who promised that they would work in Hawaii. Instead, after the long voyage, the Koreans discovered themselves in the bleak Southwest Mexican desert of Vera Cruz. In a totally strange land, Koreans were forced to work and live like slaves. With no means of getting out of their predicament, the miserable enslavement was not discovered until a Korean merchant was visiting the area. Shocked by the scene of fellow countrymen working as slaves, he immediately informed the Korean government of the situation. Upon receiving the report, the king issued a ban on Korean emigration anywhere.

Secondly, in the same year (1905), Korea became Japan's protectorate, and Japan was in full control of her foreign affairs, including emigration. The Japanese government was concerned about the potential threat of hostile Koreans to the Japanese people in Hawaii. She also saw the growing number of Koreans in Hawaii as a source of political trouble in the future.

Practice of Picture Marriage

Among the early emigrants to Hawaii, the ratio of men to women between 20 and 49 was almost 13 to 1. Many Korean bachelors were left with one of three options as far as marriage was concerned: marry a woman of another nationality (such as Hawaiian or Portuguese), return to Korea to marry at home, or rely on a marriage broker for a Korean picture bride.

The first option was not that viable due to racial prejudice on both sides. In addition, not many Korean workers were equipped to overcome language and cultural barriers. Yet some managed to marry Hawaiian and European (mainly Portuguese) women.

The second option was not that viable either. The cost of a round trip to Korea and back was beyond the reach of many workers. Also, the loss of wages during the leave of absence would be considerable. Furthermore, any proud Korean man would remain a bachelor rather than losing face by visiting home empty-handed. The round-trip fare was one thing, and the expense of a wedding and gifts for family members and relatives would be quite another. This economic factor kept many Korean workers from returning home for marriage.

The third option, a picture marriage, was the most reasonable and attractive. Without risking honor, one could marry a Korean woman at an affordable cost through the arrangement of a broker. The picture marriage gave the men distinct advantages over the women. They did not have to show their dismal physical condition—the wrinkled, tanned old face and callous hands from years of hard labor. As a matter of fact, many used the pictures they had taken of themselves in Korea many years before. Even if they might have to take pictures in Hawaii for exchange, the photographers would make them look many years younger than their actual appearance by skillful touch-ups.

Such tricks were used by both sides. Some women took advantage of the picture marriage by covering their physical handicaps. A few women with pock marks or crippled legs managed to deceive their men.

The plantation owners were also interested in promoting picture marriage in order to maintain a stable work force. Bachelor workers usually tended to cause more trouble through excessive drinking, gambling, fighting, and adultery. The absenteeism among such workers was much higher than among married workers.

With the approval of the U.S. government, the first Korean picture bride, Sara Choe, came to Hawaii on November 28, 1910. She married Lee Nae Soo. Until 1924 when the U. S. Congress passed the Oriental Exclusion Act, nearly 1,000 picture brides crossed the Pacific Ocean. Through the medium of black and white pictures, many Koreans practiced the age-honored custom of arranged marriage.

Some Korean workers were too poor to afford a simple wedding band for their brides, so they borrowed from others a gold ring, which cost about seven dollars, just for the wedding day. Only a small number of picture brides refused to marry their picture grooms. These women were taken care of by church-operated institutes. Those brides who had not known men before were more likely to stay with the old men they married. The so-called "widow picture brides," however, experienced more marital problems with their second husbands in Hawaii.

Although some picture marriages turned out happy and others not so happy, the contributions of picture brides were significant. The Korean population multiplied through these women, and the men found stability and security through family life.   In turn, this resulted in economic prosperity for many Korean families in Hawaii and the mainland.

Before the Koreans tried it, Chinese and Japanese workers in Hawaii and the mainland had used the same method of finding a spouse.

Thus the fates of Mr. Chung Bong Woon and his wife were shaped by forces on both sides of the Pacific Ocean. They thought the small island territory of America would offer a better future than did the small peninsular colony of Japan.   And they tried very hard to make their wishes come true.

NOTES

[1] The name of the last dynasty, Chosun, means morning calm.

[2] Bong Youn Choy, *Korean Americans* (Chicago: Nelson-Hall Inc., 1979), 43-49.

[3] Nigel Cameron, *From Bondage to Liberation: East Asia 1860-1952* (Hong Kong: Oxford University Press, 1975), 82-87.

[4] This was the first immigration legislation ever passed by the Congress of the United States.

[5] Wayne Patterson and Hyung-Chan Kim, *The Koreans in America* (Minneapolis: Lerner Publication Co., 1977), 17-20.

[6] Howard Brett Melendy, *Asians in America* (Boston: Twayne Publishers, 1977), 122-123.

[7] Patterson and Kim, 21-23.

[8] Choy, 75.

[9] Choy, 73.

[10] Choy, 73.

[11] Choy, 75.

12 Choy, 75-76.

13 Ronald Takaki, *Pau Hana: Plantation Life and Labor in Hawaii* (Honolulu: University of Hawaii, 1983), 66-75.

6

THE PATRIOTS

During the Korean independence movement, from 1905 to the end of Second World War (1945), Hawaii became one of a few overseas bases.   The island territory attracted common laborers by the thousands, and they formed a critical mass.   Accordingly, many prominent Korean leaders were attracted to the growing Korean communities in the islands.   The almost midpoint location of Hawaii in the Pacific Ocean also made it a popular station for many who traveled between Korea and America.   Thus, Mr. Chung and his wife met many independence-movement leaders and worked for some of them.

Those who became the movement leaders came to America for study and training.   They were largely the children of affluent families who were aware of modernization in other parts of the world.   After studying abroad, some returned to Korea and others chose to remain in America.   A number of those who remained in America dedicated their lives to the independence movement.

Of the patriotic leaders active in America, Mr. Park Yong Man and Dr. Rhee Syngman had significant personal contacts with Mr. Chung and his wife Young Oak. The two prominent figures established their own brands of independence movement in Hawaii where the largest number of Koreans were concentrated. The leaders represented different philosophies for achieving independence. Park Yong Man adopted a militaristic approach, whereas Dr. Rhee Syngman advocated political and diplomatic approaches.

Park Yong Man and his followers believed that military agitations against Japan might hasten the end of the Japanese colonial occupation of Korea. Although they were separated from home by about three thousand miles of pacific ocean, the physical distance didn't deter their spirit.

Park Yong Man provided strong leadership for those who supported the military approach. He came to America in 1904 after an aborted reform movement against the faltering Yi Dynasty. Upon graduating from the University of Nebraska, where he majored in political science and minored in military science, he set up The Korean Youth Military Academy in Hastings, Nebraska, in 1909. Twenty-seven cadets were recruited and trained in basic military drill, field tactics, and theory five evenings a week. During the day, they worked on farms to support themselves. Since the Korean cadets were aliens, it was against the law of the United States to use real rifles. Thus the academy had to substitute wooden guns for real ones in their training.[1]

Following the example of the first military academy in Nebraska, groups of former Korean soldiers set up similar training centers: two in California and one each in Kansas and Wyoming.[2]

Later a Korean pilot training program was established at Willows, California. Kim Chong Nim, a rich rice farmer in Central California, donated three airplanes to the school of aviation. Moreover, he supported the school with a monthly contribution of 3,000 dollars.[3]

The Koreans in Hawaii followed the example of their mainland counterpart. They established similar military training camps on the islands of Oahu, Maui, and Hawaii. Eventually Park Yong Man moved to Hawaii at the request of the Korean National Association, and he established the Korean National Brigade by consolidating the different camps on the Hawaiian islands. The newly consolidated military training school was located on a pineapple plantation on Oahu's windward side. Mr. Park became the head of the brigade. A total of 311 cadets, mainly ex-soldiers, received military training at night. During the day they worked on plantations.

Some Americans were uneasy about the military training programs run by Korean expatriates. They remembered the assassination of an American citizen by a Korean in San Francisco. The person assassinated was Durham White Stevens, who had been working for the Japanese government in the area of foreign affairs. - In March 1908 he was on a public relations tour in America, attempting to sway public opinion toward justifying the Japanese protectorate of Korea. His public statements in favor of Japanese policy humiliated many Koreans in the Bay area.

On the morning of March 23, two Koreans, Chun Myung Woon and Chang In Hwan, attacked Stevens as he was waiting for the train to Washington, D. C. In spite of the law prohibiting Orientals from purchasing guns, Chang managed to secure a hand-gun. While Chun was scuffling with Stevens using a toy gun, Chang shot Stevens twice. Stevens never recovered and died two days later.

On trial, Chang asked the judge for a death sentence. He would rather be martyred for his country than be imprisoned. But the judge sentenced him to serve 25 years at San Quentin State Prison.4

Resistance continued against Japanese attempts to complete the colonization of Korea. This time another Korean patriot expressed his anger in Manchuria. When the chief Japanese architect of the protectorate came to Harbin to have a conference with Russian representatives, Mr. An Joong Keun assassinated Ito Hirobumi and his entourage.

A Surprise Gift

One day Mr. Park Yong Man got a surprise contribution from a plantation worker. It was the ex-soldier, Mr. Chung Bong Woon, who gave 1,500 dollars for the military training school. The contribution was an extremely large amount, considering that the average earning of plantation workers was about 70 cents a day. It would take almost seven years of daily wages for a plantation worker to save that amount, not including bonuses. The donation was made years before Mr. Chung arranged a picture marriage.

Moved by the contribution, Mr. Park invited Mr. Chung to a dinner in honor of his generous support. For the occasion, Mr. Park chose a high-class American restaurant in Honolulu and ordered beef steak for his guests. Not being able to use fork and a knife very well, Mr. Chung gave up eating the steak after a considerable struggle. He simply could not cut the roasted beef into small pieces. On the plantation he hardly had a chance to eat American food, not to mention learning proper American table manners. He left the restaurant hungry and disgusted.

As the two were leaving the restaurant, Mr. Chung complained to Mr. Park for patronizing the American restaurant. So they went to a Korean restaurant, and Mr. Chung ordered a Korean dish that he enjoyed.

As Mr. Park became more realistic about his military approach to independence, he became greatly interested in Korean military activities in China. In order to stay closer to Korea and her enemy, he went to China. But in Peking on October 17, 1928, his life was ended prematurely by an assassin's bullet.

Mr. Chung's anti-Japanese sentiment was beyond all doubt. For instance, he never allowed any of his family members to wear Japanese-style slippers. He also ordered his wife not to speak Japanese under any circumstance. Fearing her husband, his wife would use hand and body gestures to communicate at Japanese stores. Realizing that the Korean woman understood what they were saying, the Japanese clerks would speak to her in Japanese anyway. He would whip his boys if they were found playing with Japanese toys, singing Japanese songs, or wearing Japanese clothes. (A few Korean women's organizations both in Hawaii and on the mainland launched an anti-Japanese products campaign.) The ex-Korean soldier never forgave Japan for occupying his country.

Young Oak's Lifelong Mentor

Young Oak's association with Dr. Rhee Syngman lasted almost half a century. It began in 1918 when she came to Hawaii and endured until his death in Hawaii in 1965. Dr. Rhee became the most influential figure in shaping Young Oak's political views and social activities. She was very loyal and faithful to the leader who never forgot her patriotic service.

Rhee Syngman was born on March 26, 1875, in Hwanghae Province (now in North Korea). At the age of 23, the liberal-minded Rhee Syngman was sentenced to death for the crime of advocating the end of the Yi Dynasty. Luckily, he was released in 1904, and he went to the United States. Upon arrival, he entered George Washington University. After graduation he continued his education at Harvard University, where he earned a master's degree in 1908. In 1910, he received a Ph.D. from Princeton University, thus receiving the first Ph.D. ever conferred upon a Korean by an American university.

He came to Hawaii at the request of his former prison-mate, Park Yong Man. They were comrades in the new movement they led against the old-fashioned Yi Dynasty. After his arrival, Hawaii became a base for Dr. Rhee's independence movement. Many Korean residents there, if not all, supported him throughout his political career.

Mr. Chung Bong Woon and his wife were associated with Dr. Rhee Syngman mainly through two of his organizations: The Korean Christian Church and Dong-Ji Hoi (The Comrade Society). The two became Dr. Rhee's main political instruments to promote the independence movement. For many years, the couple's social activities evolved around the two organizations.

Dr. Rhee realized the strong influence of the Christian church among Koreans in Hawaii. He insisted that religious freedom should precede political freedom. He argued that there was no reason for Korean Christians to be controlled by an American denomination. So he started the Korean Christian Church in December 1918, completely independent of any major denominations. There was strong opposition to such a move among Korean members of the mainline denominations.5 People called it "The Independent Church."

When Young Oak came to Maui, Dr. Rhee's proposal for the establishment of the Korean Christian Church was circulating. Mr. Chung embraced the proposal without a second thought, but Mrs. Chung maintained that she should attend the Methodist Church. Her reason was simple and practical. She thought that the new church did not have much to offer for religious growth and development. This angered her husband. Eventually Young Oak yielded to the wish of her husband, and this became a turning-point in her political involvement.

Not long after the establishment of the independent church, in July 1921, Dr. Rhee launched his own political organization the Dong-Ji Hoi (The Comrade Society). The society was a rival of the mainstream Korean National Association.

Its goal was to protect the Korean Provisional Government-in-exile by assisting the chairman (Dr. Rhee Syngman) in his execution of policies. The society demanded absolute obedience from its members, and any deviation from the rules of the society would be duly dealt with.6

Dr. Rhee also established the Korean Christian Institute to educate the children of Korean residents. The institute was to prepare Korean youths for the coming independence of their motherland. It offered courses in Korean language, history, and culture. In addition, the school taught English and Western civilization.

The March First Movement

While overseas Koreans launched various organizational efforts to regain independence, Koreans at home were secretly preparing for a nationwide demonstration. The political volcano finally erupted throughout the country on March First, 1919. In response to the Principle of Autonomous Rule advocated by President Woodrow Wilson after the First World War, the leaders of the Korean independence movement proclaimed the Declaration of Independence. The people at home burst into the streets of large cities crying for independence from the colonial rule of Japan. It was a bloody protest movement that lost many lives through the bullets and swords of Japanese troops and policemen.

Koreans in Hawaii responded to the March First movement at home. Obtaining the plan and a copy of the Declaration of Independence through Korean agents in China, Hawaiian Koreans poured into the streets of Honolulu shouting for independence. Before they marched to the street, they heard the Declaration of Independence.7

We herewith proclaim the independence of Korea and the liberty of the Korean people. We tell it to the world in witness of the equality of all nations, and we pass it on to our posterity as their inherent right.

We make this proclamation, having back of us a history of forty-three centuries and 20,000,000 united, loyal people. We take this step to insure to our children for all time to come, life and liberty in accord with the awakening conscience of this new era. This is the clear leading of God, the moving principle of the present age, the just claim of the whole human race. It is something that cannot be stamped out, stifled, or gagged, or suppressed by any means.

Victims of an older age, when brute force and the spirit of plunder ruled, we have come after these long thousands of years to experience the agony of ten years of foreign oppression, with every loss of the right to live, every restriction of the freedom of thought, every damage done to the dignity of life, every opportunity lost for a share in the intelligent advance of the age in which we live.

Assuredly, if the defects of the past are to be rectified, if the wrongs of the present are to be righted, if future oppression is to be avoided, if thought is to be set free, if right of action is to be given a place, if we are to attain to any way of progress, if we are to deliver our children from the painful heritage of shame, if we are to leave blessing and happiness intact for those who succeed us, the first of all necessary things is the complete independence of our people. What cannot our twenty millions do, with hearts consecrated to liberty, in this day when human nature and conscience are making a stand for truth and right? What barrier can we not break, what purpose can we not accomplish?

We have no desire to accuse Japan of breaking many solemn treaties since 1876, nor to single out specially the teachers in the schools or the Government officials who treat the heritage of our ancestors as a colony of their own, and our people and our civilization as a nation of savages, and who delight only in beating us down and bringing us under their heel.

We have no wish to find special fault with Japan's lack of fairness or her contempt for our civilization and the principles on which her state rests; we, who have greater cause to reprimand ourselves, need not spend time in finding fault with others; neither need we, who require so urgently to build for the future, spend useless hours over what is past and gone. Our urgent need today is the rebuilding of this house of ours and not the discussion of who has broken it down, or what has caused its ruin. Our work is to clear the future of defects in accord with the earnest dictates of conscience. Let us not be filled with bitterness or resentment over past agonies or past occasions for anger.

Our part is to influence the Japanese government, dominated as it is by the old idea of brute force which thinks to run counter to reason and universal law, so that it will change and act honestly and in accord with the principles of right and truth.

The result of annexation, brought about against the will of the Korean people, is that the Japanese are concerned only for their own gain, and by a false set of figures show a profit and loss account between us two peoples most untrue, digging a trench of everlasting resentment deeper and deeper the farther they go.

Ought not the way of enlightened courage to be to correct the evils of the past by ways that are sincere, and by true sympathy and friendly feelings make a new world in which the two peoples will be equally blessed?

To bind by force twenty millions of resentful Koreans will mean not only loss of peace forever for this part of the Far East, but also will increase the ever-growing suspicions of four hundred millions of Chinese--upon whom depends the safety of the Far East--besides strengthening the hatred of Japan. From this all the rest of the East will suffer. Today Korean independence will mean not only life and happiness for us, but also Japan's departure from an evil path and her exaltation to the place of true protector of the East, so that China too would put all fear of Japan aside. This thought comes from no minor resentment, but from a large hope for the future welfare and blessings of mankind.

A new era wakes before our eyes, the old world of force is gone, and the new world of righteousness and truth is here. Out of the experience and travail of the old world arises this light on the affairs of life. Insects stifled by their foe, the snows of winter, are also awakened at this time of the year by the breezes of spring and the warm light of the snow upon them.

It is the day of the restoration of all things, on the full tide of which we set forth without delay or fear. We desire a full measure of satisfaction in the way of life, liberty and the pursuit of happiness, and an opportunity to develop what is in us for the glory of our people. In this hope we go forward.

To this paean of praise for a new age of enlightened justice which the Korean leadership felt was being ushered in by Woodrow Wilson with his Charter of the Fourteen Points, the Committee of Thirty-three added a three-fold injunction for the Mansei demonstrators:

1. This work of ours is in behalf of truth, justice, and life, undertaken at the request of our people,

in order to make known their desire for liberty. Let no violence be done to anyone.

2. Let those who follow us show every hour with gladness this same spirit.

3. Let all things be done with singleness of purpose, so that our behavior to the very end may be honorable and upright.

Dated the 4252d Year of the Kingdom of Korea, 3d Month, 1st Day.

The message of the Declaration of Independence was powerful. At the same time, it reminded its listeners of the sad fate of their country and people.

Wearing costumes and holding the national flag, Koreans on Oahu marched orderly from King Street to Waikiki. The spectators in the street applauded the demonstrators, and many threw coins and bills onto the Korean flag as an expression of support.

Some Koreans took this as an opportunity to express their patriotism in public. At the same time, it was an opportunity to vent their collective frustration and disappointment.

During the demonstration, a man by the name of Bang Dal Moon cut off the tip of his index finger. This illiterate, experiencing a severe pain, asked the other demonstrators to write "Independence of Korea" on a white bed sheet with his dripping red blood. As soon as the demonstrators held up the banner of fresh blood, many choked. Such a brave act by a plantation worker surprised even fellow Koreans who had never thought him so patriotic.

Not long after the March demonstration, a Korean bachelor became depressed about the future of his country. He could not see the end of colonial rule at home, so he decided to end his own existence. The Korean man was rescued by fellow countrymen when he tried to commit a protest suicide by pressing his abdomen upon a sharp knife. Unable to recover from the serious wound, he died a few months later.

The suicide attempt reminded many Koreans of Lee Jun who went to the Netherlands to attend the Second Hague Peace Conference in May 1907. It was a secret mission arranged by the desperate Korean Emperor, Ko Jong. Under the pressure of Japan, other nations did not officially recognize the Korean delegates. The frustrated Korean delegate, Lee Jun, protested against the Japanese protectorate by killing himself.

In response to the March First Movement at home, Mr. Ahn Chang Ho, the chairman of the Korean National Association, made an appeal to American Christians.8

A Korean Appeal to America

We, the representatives of Korea, in this hour of her dire need, issue to you, our fellow-Christians and citizens of the world's foremost Power, an appeal for justice and humanity.

In great trouble, after prayer to Almighty God, we have turned to you as our only refuge.

For ten years we have been oppressed by a militaristic and imperialistic Government. With no more right than Germany when she crushed Belgium under her heel and brought down upon herself the condemnation of Christendom, the Japanese Government has not only robbed us of national liberty, but has deprived us of those rights which are the heritage of every human being. It has deprived us of justice, of freedom of thought, of our language, of the right to educate our children according to our ideals, imposing upon us a system of education not only destructive of our national ideals, but imperilling the very foundations of the Christian religion.

They have also taken from us the sacred right of religious freedom. The Christians have been the repeated objects of brutal and nation-wide persecution and oppression, many having suffered imprisonment and barbarous and inhuman treatment without any just cause.

The story of the numerous outbursts of cruelty, of the wholesale slaughterings, of the systematic oppression which has employed every form of inhumanity, which has not only robbed our people of their very homes but has made it almost impossible for many to make a living, driving them to desperation and starvation, and of the cunning press which kept the truth from the world by flaunting in its eyes a story of material progress, is a tragedy and pathetic tale which cries out before God and humanity.

At last our race has arisen and proclaimed to the world, in no mistaken terms, its desire for liberty and for freedom from oppression and unbearable tyranny. No force has been employed. The new movement in Korea which has attracted the attention of the world is no more than a legitimate and spontaneous expression of a national conviction.

But the Japanese have replied with force and brutality. The Christian church in Korea, especially, has become again the centre of barbarous persecution. Christians have been made to bear crosses in mockery of their religion, while the name of Christ has been subjected to infamy. A little girl who held up the proclamations of independence in her hands had her arms severed. Thousands have been imprisoned and tortured; thousands have been killed. Can the Christian church in America stand passively by without even raising a voice in protest?

The hour for Korea has struck, and the fate of Christ's kingdom in our country hangs in the balance, for even religion cannot withstand this fatal process of denationalization and deracination.

The great war has ushered in a new day for the human race. With ten millions of lives the world has bought freedom from autocracy and militarism. The right of self-determination has been declared universal. The world has been rejoicing over the incoming of a new era when international oppression and injustice are to be known no more, an era in which the rights of small nationalities are to be protected by a world League of Nations.

To you, citizens of that nation which has been the leader in this epoch-making movement, we appeal. Are the principles of the world's new League mere shibboleths, or are they joyous proclamations of a new day on earth? Do they apply only to Europe, or are they world-wide in their scope? Has the world defeated militarism and imperialism in Germany only to let it stalk its bloody and untrammeled course in the Far East? Surely not. And surely America will not, can not, stand by and let us suffer. At least the Christian churches of America will lift a voice in protest and in appeal that justice be done, and that those principles for which so many precious American lives were sacrificed shall become the heritage of the world, shall be operative not only in Europe but in the Far East, shall usher in for Korea, too, a new day of justice and freedom from oppression.

Patriotic Campaigns

The March First Movement left a strong impression in the mind of Young Oak who had left Korea about one year before. The experience stirred her patriotism. She decided to be a part of the independence movement, and she worked hard for Dr. Rhee's Comrade Society. From then on she responded to the call of duty for her church and the Comrade Society.

The Korean women in Hawaii wanted to help the independence movement. They started the Korean Women Relief Society with 300 charter members. Young Oak became the secretary of its Maui branch. She did much fund raising, remission, and record keeping to support the independence movement.

The members did many things to raise funds. For instance, each family would save a few ounces of rice every day in a designated bag. Once a month the women got together and made cakes with the rice they had saved. The proceeds of the rice cake sale were sent to the Korean Provisional Government in exile.

One time they were bold enough to put on a show in a theater for the purpose of raising funds. Without any professional supervision, they made up a story about an ancient Korean king and his life in the palace. The intent was to show Korean customs. They rented a local theater for 75 dollars. The admission charge was one dollar, and more than 150 tickets were sold.

But the drama was slow and boring. Other than the colorful homemade costumes, nothing was interesting. Even Koreans in the audience began to complain. People shouted "boos" and cat-calls. Many so-called actors could not remember their lines. The show was a total disaster.

To avoid further embarrassment, Young Oak and others extemporaneously started playing a Korean folk dance. It was a singing dialogue between a beggar and his patrons. The audience was at least listening to vivacious music and movement. They began throwing coins at the actors who had played the begging scene. When the women collected the coins, the amount totaled 17 dollars.

On many occasions, the young mother was on the road to collect free-will contributions for the Korean Independence Movement, carrying a baby on her back and holding the hand of another boy. She went from one plantation to another. But the poor Korean plantation workers could donate only one or two quarters. They felt sorry for her, but they couldn't help.

Often the mother and her babies skipped meals during the fund-raising trip. The baby would bite the mother's nipple, which did not produce sufficient milk. To the crying baby, the mother would say in a choked voice. "Since you are a son of Korea, you suffer as much as your parents. But we have to endure this suffering until the day of independence."

One day during a fund-raising tour, Young Oak stopped at an old plantation worker's house. The man donated 50 cents. In order to register the contribution in the record book, she asked the man's name.

"What is your name?"

The old man was very angry at her because she did not use a proper expression in her question.

"What kind of woman are you? Who is your husband? Don't you know how to address an older person in a respectful way?" The offended old man was furious.

Ashamed, Young Oak replied, "Sir, I am sorry for not knowing the proper way of speaking to an older person. Since I came to Hawaii as a picture bride when I was 16, I haven't had the chance to learn proper manners. Please forgive my ignorance and impoliteness. Please teach me the proper way of addressing an old man." Then she cried before the old man out of self-pity.

Since that experience, Young Oak never forgot the proper manner of asking an older person questions. In the meantime, Mr. Chung was willing to put up with the inconvenience of his wife's absence for days. He hired temporary help for cooking and washing. The couple endured hardships to regain the independence of their country.

NOTES

[1] Bong Youn Choy, *Korean Americans* (Chicago: Nelson-Hall Inc., 1979), 85.

[2] Choy, 85.

[3] Hyung-Chan Kim and Wayne Patterson, *The Koreans in America 1882-1974: A Chronology and Fact Book* (Dobbs Ferry: Oceana Publications, Inc., 1974), 32.

[4] Kim and Patterson, 27.

[5] Choy, 146-149.

[6] Kim and Patterson, 101.

[7] Robert T. Oliver, *Syngman Rhee: The Man Behind the Myth* (New York: Dodd Mead and Co., 1954), 136-138.

[8] Chang-ho Ahn, "A Korean Appeal to America," *The Nation*, vol. 108, No. 2807, April 19, 1919, pp. 638-639.

7

THE RISE OF THE FAMILY

After the birth of her last baby, Ronald, in 1930, Mrs. Chung began to experience terrible physical weakness. She lost her appetite, was often struck by severe dizzy spells, and became very depressed. Apparently, giving birth to six boys every other year had taken a severe toll on her. The mother had nursed the six babies without sufficient time to replenish her strength. Moreover, taking care of the boys was an extraordinarily demanding task. The enormous amount of cooking, washing, cleaning, and sewing for the growing family was done by her two hands. There was no one around to help the young mother during her pregnancies and the subsequent care of the children.

One day, a couple of Filipino plantation workers came to Young Oak's house with an armful of soiled clothes. They mistook Mrs. Chung for a laundry lady because they saw lines of clothes hanging in her front yard every time they passed by.

By this time, her homesickness was getting worse. It had been more than 15 years since she had left Korea. She was so homesick that she would do almost anything in order to see her parents. The letters she was receiving from home did not help.

Since her illness was getting worse, Mr. Chung had his wife see the plantation physician, who diagnosed her illness as low blood pressure and anemia due to malnutrition. He ordered Mrs. Chung to check in immediately at the Queen's Hospital in Honolulu. There, in spite of three expensive blood transfusions, she did not recover. Many times Mrs. Chung thought that she was dying. What made her really sad was not the fear of her own premature death in a foreign country but that her parents and her six boys would be left behind. Such imaginary self-pity didn't help her recover.

Overwhelmed by self-pity, she sometimes cried day and night. She wished that she had not been born. She pictured herself as someone who had come to the unfamiliar island to marry a stranger when she was only 16 and dying so young after years of loneliness and hardship on the desolate plantation. All of a sudden, she saw her life as a flower bud withering unexpectedly before it had a chance to fully bloom. Even the chirpings of the birds she could see through the hospital window seemed to be a call to immediate death.

During the long hospitalization at the Queen's Hospital from January 1934 to March 1935, many Korean members of the Comrade Society visited her. One day one of the visitors gave her a book titled *Religion of New Life* written by the famous Japanese Christian, Kakawa Toyohiko.

The book inspired Mrs. Chung tremendously. She read it over and over again. According to Toyohiko, one's happiness in life depends on his or her perception of reality. If one takes an optimistic perspective, one is happy regardless of external conditions. On the other hand, if one takes a pessimistic view, one is going to be miserable. She gained new insight on life and faith. Her despair and melancholy suddenly faded away. It was like seeing calm sunlight after a violent storm. She began to feel strong, and she regained her appetite. Now the birds around the hospital seemed to sing for her quick recovery. The trees and flowers appeared to wave at her as they were touched by an ocean breeze.

One day, her doctor at the Queen's Hospital suggested that she visit Korea. He assured her that she could make the long voyage. Young Oak could not believe the suggestion. All of a sudden, she felt like flying.

Mr. Chung took the doctor's recommendation seriously. After losing almost all hope that his young wife would recover, he decided to let her try the voyage and the Oriental medical treatment at home. He reasoned that if she were to die, she should at least see her parents before anything happened.

Mr. Chung arranged everything for his wife's home visit. A few days before her scheduled departure, he came to the hospital. He brought with him only the two older boys.

"Don't worry about us here," he encouraged. "We will manage all right. You stay in Korea at least six months, or longer if necessary. I hope we will see you return happy and healthy."

He tried to comfort his wife. Harry gave his mother a small metal cross, telling her that she should remember Jesus whenever she was not feeling well. They returned to Maui that same day.

Young Oak surprised her husband and the children when she came home unexpectedly the next morning. She was determined to see all her children before she was to leave. It took about eight hours each way by ferry. She cooked breakfast for the family and kissed each boy before going. On her return trip to Honolulu, she took the oldest boy with her to enroll him at a city school.

On the return to Honolulu, she was elated with the idea of visiting Korea. At the same time, she felt sorry for the little boys without their mother's care, not sure if she would see them again.

Homecoming

After 17 years away from home, Young Oak boarded a ship bound for Japan. It was April 4, 1935. Once aboard, her spirit turned buoyant like the floating ship. She was as happy as a little child and enjoyed every moment of the passage. The thought of seeing her parents, brothers, and sisters overwhelmed her. Through the years, she had heard of nothing but the success and prosperity of her family. All of her brothers and one of her sisters had finished their college education in Japan, and each of them was doing well. Young Oak was anxious to see the benefits her picture marriage had conferred upon the family.

While other passengers were suffering from terrible seasickness, Young Oak didn't experience any. Her appetite was good and she ate many of the Korean delicacies others had brought. The fresh ocean air, a strong appetite, and a joyous spirit helped her regain the weight she had lost.

Once in a while a Korean teenager on the ship reminded her of her boys at home. He was being sent to his grandparents in Korea for delinquent behavior. The boy's parents hoped that the arrangement might change their son. Yet Young Oak could not understand how parents could send their child away for any reason.

Upon her arrival at Yokohama, she was met by her brother. He was a high-ranking customs officer and made the entrance procedure short and brief for his sister and the other Korean passengers. The grateful brother treated his sister like a queen. He repeatedly told her that the family owed its success to her sacrifice. The youngest brother was assigned to escort his sister while she was in Japan and Korea. For this assignment, he took a leave of absence from his study.

After a few days of rest at her brother's family, she boarded a ship bound for Korea. On the ship, she became very emotional. Seventeen years ago, she had crossed the Korean Straits alone. Then she was only 16 years old. Now the 33-year-old lady wondered how much her motherland had changed during the years. She thought of the Korean saying, "In ten years even the shape of mountains and rivers change."

As she traveled from Pusan to Ham An by wagon, she noticed that the mountains and rivers looked the same as when she had left. However, the mountains covered with azaleas looked more beautiful than the mountains of Hawaii. The smell of colorful spring flowers and the sound of singing birds were overwhelming to the homecoming Ham An girl.

Coincidentally, it was market day when Young Oak came home. The town folk had heard of the return of Young Oak, and they lingered around her parents' house. By this time, Young Oak's parents were enjoying the wealth and fame brought by their children who had gone abroad either for marriage or study. Their house was the best in Ham An.

Young Oak's mother was relieved when she saw her daughter healthy and in good spirits. The mother expected to see her daughter in terrible condition, lingering between life and death.

This time Young Oak did not restrain herself and cried with her mother. The joy of seeing her family after 17 years of separation was overwhelming. In Young Oak's cry, there were many stories that she did not want to disclose to anyone. Those who witnessed the scene could not help but shed tears of their own.

Always generous and large-minded, Young Oak asked her mother to buy all the delicacies the women had brought to sell in the market. It didn't take many dollars to buy them, no more than 75 dollars. Young Oak's mother reminded her daughter of the ridicules and contempt they had endured at the time of her picture engagement. But Young Oak didn't mind that at all. "Mother, it is good to share good things with others. I would rather be in the position of giving than receiving."

Everyone was invited to join the family in a celebration of her visit. People stared at Young Oak and touched her as if she were a foreigner. They whispered that the former Ham An girl looked somewhat different from them, and they speculated that the different water and food of Hawaii might have changed her considerably.

The scene was quite a contrast to the time when Young Oak had left Ham An as a picture bride. Instead of pitying the daughter of poor parents, people had seen what the picture bride had done for her family over the years. So the townsfolk happily compared Young Oak to Shim Chung, who had returned as a queen and at whose party her father's eyesight had been restored.

Young Oak's parents took her to the best herb doctors around Ham An. They concluded that Young Oak had been exposed to cold air too soon after one of her deliveries. This reminded Young Oak of the sudden chill all over her body as she had come home from the hospital after the birth of her first baby. Later she had been hospitalized again for about three months. But she knew well that the underlying cause of her illness was exhaustion and unbearable loneliness. All these years her daily sleep and diet were far from adequate.

Accordingly, one of the herb doctors prescribed a special treatment. It worked effectively, and she seemed to rapidly regain strength and warmth. She had rediscovered the value of living with her parents and siblings. The moment she saw her family, she seemed to regain vitality and hope. Moreover, seeing the results of her own sacrifice for the family gave her tremendous satisfaction. Her picture marriage and the hardships she had endured in Hawaii had brought good fortune to the family.

Nevertheless, she told herself repeatedly that she would never let any of her children or their children marry at a young age. She believed that children should stay with their parents as long as possible.

During her visit, she met one of the two Ham An girls she had induced into the picture marriage. It was Lee Sunhee. When Lee Sunhee had met her husband in Hawaii, she had been quite disappointed. Nor could she stand the monotonous plantation life. In a few months she became pregnant but she insisted on returning to Korea. Thus her picture marriage lasted just six months.

At the time Young Oak was visiting Ham An, Lee Sunhee was living alone in poverty with a teenage daughter from the marriage. What made Young Oak feel bad was that the poor woman had become blind. When Young Oak scolded the former picture bride for her impatience, she replied only with sighs and tears. Lee Sunhee could not say much to Young Oak, who had made a worse match a success.

Another friend, Yim Subi, had become as pitiful as Lee Sunhee. Not long after her marriage to a plantation worker, Yim Subi had discovered that her husband had a severe case of tuberculosis. Soon he was taken to a sanitarium where he died within a year. She remarried. The last thing Young Oak heard about Yim Subi was that she had five children. After that, Young Oak lost touch with her friend forever.

Young Oak now had mixed feelings about the picture marriage. She felt sorry for her two friends whose marriages had turned out failures. If she had not pushed for the picture marriage, her two friends would have married Ham An boys and lived happily staying close to their families. They might have had to struggle to survive, but they wouldn't have had to go through the misery of living in a foreign country. Their human sufferings in Hawaii had outweighed the meager benefits of the plantation life. The young girls had never estimated the gravity of loneliness, homesickness, and plantation life. After all, Hawaii had been no more than a mirage to the poor Ham An girls.

Young Oak could not say many good things about her own marriage either. Other than watching and hoping for her six growing boys, she didn't find much pleasure in life. The young wife had been deprived of even the joy of intimate relationship after her husband's accident on the job. Although her family was not struggling as badly as some other Korean families on the plantations, there was no guaranteed economic security for the future. As long as Mr. Chung was healthy and diligent, the family would be fed and clothed.

New Beginning

With the utmost care of her parents and siblings, Young Oak's recuperation was speedy. She had regained both mental and physical strength. One day, while Young Oak was lying in a thick silk quilt, a strange woman came into the house with her baby on her back. The pitiful woman was begging for food for her starving child. As she looked at Young Oak, the woman murmured, "What a lucky woman she is. She looks like an angel from paradise."

The woman's words struck Young Oak hard. All of a sudden, the faces of her six boys and her old husband flashed before her. The rest and comfort she was experiencing at her parents' home made her feel guilty as she thought of her own family in Hawaii. Young Oak reflected that the woman with a child on her back was luckier than she who had left six boys in a faraway land. She missed them much.

In spite of her husband's suggestion to stay at least six months, she decided to return to Hawaii after four months. Her parents did not try to change her mind because they had heard her calling the children's names in her sleep almost every night. The parents realized how much their daughter missed her family. In a letter to his wife, Mr Chung said that he had lost his job as a locomotive maintenance man. Therefore, he had no choice but to move to Honolulu in the near future. He said that workers continued to lose jobs because of the effects of the Great Depression.

As Young Oak thought of the family's future in Honolulu, she became apprehensive. At the same time, she welcomed the excuse for a change. She had become tired of humdrum plantation life. Furthermore, physically demanding labor was becoming too much for her husband who was approaching sixty.

Another important reason for welcoming the change was the education of the boys. She thought that the secondary schools around the plantation were not so good as the city schools in Honolulu.

Yet, she painfully realized that she and her husband had no viable means of supporting themselves in the city. Neither of them had education or skills marketable in Honolulu. Moreover, Mr. Chung, the sole breadwinner, was too old to be gainfully employed in the city after so many years of plantation labor.

The considerate daughter didn't tell anyone her predicament. She didn't want to hurt the feelings of her parents. No one in Ham An could ever imagine the hard life and uncertainty she was facing in Hawaii. They all believed that Young Oak was happily married to a well-to-do Korean who had demonstrated his wealth during the picture engagement.

So she decided to start a venture herself. As the day of her return approached, she bought dry food and other Korean goods for her future grocery store in Honolulu.

Saying good-bye to her old parents was painful. Her mother was 60 and her father 70. She was not sure whether she would see them again. But she was grateful to be one of the few who could afford such a visit. She knew many Korean women who had come to Hawaii as picture brides were barely making ends meet. To them, visiting home to see their loved ones, not to mention returning a heroine, was a mere dream.

This time, Young Oak's voyage back to Hawaii was not so uncertain as the first one. Now she knew who would be waiting for her and what she could expect. Besides a husband of 17 years, she was anxious to see the six boys who were so precious to her. Having been away from them a few months, she realized for the first time that her life would be almost empty and meaningless without them. She would make any sacrifice for their future.

As soon as she returned to Honolulu, she rented a house for a family residence and a grocery store. Then she had Mr. Chung and the boys move to Honolulu for a new start.

Around this time, Mr. Chung was one of a few remaining Korean plantation workers. Many Koreans had left the plantation after a few years of work. The majority moved to Honolulu, the San Francisco Bay area and its vicinity, and Southern California. From the beginning, Mr. Chung ruled out going to the mainland. He kept saying that no place could beat Hawaii for weather and natural beauty. Also, the make-up of Hawaiian population, especially the sizable oriental population, made him feel at ease. His big family made him concerned to have a reliable and steady income rather than to venture into a new business in a big city. The language barrier and old age made him very cautious. Were it not for the Great Depression, perhaps he would have worked all his active years around the plantation.

The grocery store Young Oak started didn't do well. People had little money to spend. Many were out of work. Much of the food she brought from Korea to sell was devoured by the boys. The amount of food consumed by the growing boys was amazing. After five months she had no choice but to close down the money-losing store.

Having no other means of supporting the family, Young Oak managed to find a job for her husband on a newly established pineapple plantation on the island of Lanai. During the summer, Mr. Chung and his sons earned $800. At the end of the summer, the mother and the boys returned to Honolulu for school, and the father remained on the plantation.

Young Oak separated her six boys into two bedrooms: three skinny ones in one bedroom and three fat boys in the other. The noise in the house was deafening, and war never ceased between the two rooms. Anyone trying to find the Chung residence had only to ask for the family with boys, and the neighbors knew it right away. When the family moved away from 1515 Pele Street, the neighbors declared the street a Ghost Town.

Rise After Pearl Harbor

It is ironic that the fall of Pearl Harbor in December 1941 was a chance for many Korean families in Honolulu to rise economically. While Japanese Americans suffered a great deal from anti-Japanese attitude of the American public, many Koreans took the occasion to rally for the independence of their motherland. The Koreans in Hawaii did everything they could lest they should be misidentified as Japanese. Some went so far as to wear a button saying "I am Korean" or "I'm not Jap," and the women put on Chima Jugori to display their national origin.

Such a reaction was not limited to Hawaii. The Korean National Association of Los Angeles passed the following resolutions.

1. Koreans shall promote unity during the war and act harmoniously.

2. Koreans shall work for the defense of the country where they reside and all those who are healthy should volunteer for national guard duty. Those who are financially capable should purchase war bonds and those who are skilled should volunteer for appropriate duties.

3. Koreans shall wear a badge identifying them as Koreans, for security reasons.1

The Japanese attack on Pearl Harbor left tremendous destruction, and the salvage work demanded every available hand twenty-four hours a day. Determined to rebuild the Pacific naval power, the U. S. government poured money into Hawaii. Furthermore, the exclusion of Japanese descendants from the defense work for security reasons created a severe labor shortage.

Mr. Chung and his sons worked as much as they could. At the peak of their employment by the U.S. government, they grossed together over $5,000 a month. This brought in unexpected cash income far beyond their normal earning range. The family accumulated sizable savings, and later it became capital for the furniture manufacturing business the brothers started after the war.

The Twentieth Century Furniture Manufacturing Company was conceived by William who had been trained as a carpenter. Later, when the company grew into a major firm in Honolulu, Harry, Richard, and Ronald joined William in the operation and management of the family enterprise. Not long after the Chung family became financially secure, Walter and Robert (third and fourth in birth order) enrolled at Loma Linda University in Physical Therapy and Medicine. Gradually the success of the family business brought wealth and fame to the Chungs in Honolulu.

The proud father in his seventies would go to the factory everyday and do any chore gladly. Often he complained to his sons about the idleness of their employees. He hated waste in any form and meticulously piled the odds and ends of wood he collected from the plant floor. The disciplined old soldier and hard-working former plantation worker saw life as something to achieve rather than to enjoy.

Branching Out

As the sons grew older, the Chung family began to branch out. Harry and Walter married Korean girls whose parents were old family acquaintances. Robert married a white girl whom he met at a private college in Northern California when they were premed students. Surprisingly, the staunch nationalistic father did not object to his son's marriage to the white girl.

When William, the second son, dated an Hawaiian-born Japanese girl, the father did not raise any objection either. He said that the most important aspects of a person were character and abilities rather than ancestry.

William married the Japanese girl after his father's death. Even if Mr. Chung, who once forbade his wife to speak Japanese under any circumstance, had attended William's wedding, he would have been kind to the family members of his daughter-in-law. He would have loved William's wife as much as he loved his own son.

This was an amazing change considering how strongly anti-Japanese he was. He had forbidden any of his family members to use Japanese products around the house. (Even his Japanese daughters-in-law have been sensitive to the family norms.) Perhaps the 50-year residence in Hawaii had mellowed the stubborn old patriot. It was also possible that his Korean heritage considerably melted in the Hawaiian melting-pot. Or possibly his affection for the children overrode his personal prejudice.

The last two sons also married Japanese women. Thus, three of Mr. Chung's six sons married Japanese women whose parents' country their father so hated. Only two married Korean women. That was the magic of Hawaii and the healing power of time.

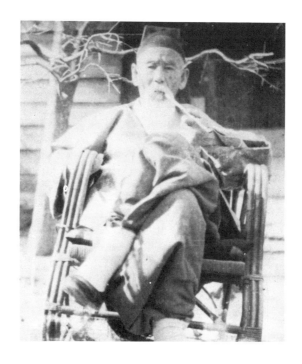

Mrs. Chung's father in 1935

Mrs. Chung with her mother (1935)

Mrs. Chung at her first visit in 1935

8

DEATH OF A
PATRIARCH

Knowing the hardships their parents went through in
their early years in Hawaii, the sons purchased a brand-
new Chrysler for the parents. For the first time in their
marriage, the couple became free from work and worry.
Mrs. Chung tried to please her old husband by driving him
around Oahu. But Mr. Chung was too old to enjoy the
driving much. He often complained of fatigue after a few
hours of sightseeing.

Once the sons made reservations for their parents at
the best resort hotels in the Hawaii islands. The trip was
meant to be a special treat. The parents were given blank
checks and credit cards for unlimited use to enjoy the islands. Whenever the young wife led her husband in and
out of expensive dining rooms and hotel lobbies, they were
mistaken for a wealthy Chinese couple. A few times, Mrs.
Chung overheard the curious guests whisper that the
young woman must be either a mistress or a legitimate wife

who married the Chinese millionaire just for his money. Others congratulated the couple assuming that they were celebrating their wedding anniversary.   However, Mr. Chung was somewhat annoyed by the unusual attention he and his wife were getting.

During the tour, they stayed at a cozy mountain-top cottage on the island of Hawaii.   One evening, while the wood was cracking in the fireplace, the wife became romantic.

"Father, I feel cold.   Please come and hold me tight." Even at that romantic moment, Mrs. Chung could not call her husband otherwise.   But Mr. Chung was sitting by the fireplace expressionless.

"Some picture brides didn't let their husbands touch them for as long as three years.   I was different.   I expected you to undress me on the first night.   My mother told me that the groom would do this.   To my disappointment, however, you asked me to change clothes myself behind the folding screen."   Young Oak wanted to provoke her husband to get a response from him.

"Now you blame me.   When I tried to touch you, you were shaking like a little deer.   How could I force a little child?"

To the repeated appeals of his wife, Mr. Chung turned to his wife on the bed and said,   "You know I am a man in appearance only.   I feel sorry for you."   Then he heaved a heavy sigh.   Mr. Chung finally stood up and embraced his wife, and that was the first embrace ever between them.

The couple painfully remembered the two accidents on the plantation that had made Mr. Chung permanently impotent.   His wife was barely 30 years old when the first accident occurred.   It was very difficult for the couple, especially for the young wife.   Besides the absence of an intimate physical relationship, Mr. Chung was not an explicitly affectionate man.   He had been brought up in Korea according to the strict Confucian code.   He had learned to keep his feelings, whether of happiness or sadness, to himself.   He believed self-control to be the sign of a virtuous man. Moreover, the considerable age difference between the two reinforced the rigid relationship. To Mr. Chung, his wife was a child, not an adult.

But the two were bound by a strong sense of respect, gratitude, and fidelity. Also, their Christian faith helped them overcome any marital dissatisfaction. Their energy and concerns were concentrated on the rearing of their six precious boys.

As a matter of fact, Mrs. Chung always advised other Korean picture brides to get along with their husbands, regardless of any unsatisfactory conditions in their married life. She admonished them to be faithful to their husbands and children. She had seen many picture brides who moved from one man to another end up in a much worse situation for themselves and their children. She saw some families whose children had each been fathered by a different man. In such families, discord and conflict ruined both parents and children.

She would often say to other picture brides, "If we had been born into rich families, we would not have come to Hawaii as picture brides. Since our families were poor, we chose to marry these men. Let us help our husbands so that we can raise our children successfully."

Death of the Patriarch

In spite of his children's efforts to please their father in his old age, Mr. Chung's health rapidly deteriorated. As Mr. Chung began to lose weight, he experienced difficulty in swallowing food. His physician son, Robert, diagnosed a malignant tumor in his father's throat. Robert knew that his father had only a few months to live. Yet he suggested to his mother that an operation might prolong the father's life a little. Mrs. Chung gave her consent, but the operation did not help much.

After the operation, Robert had his father stay at his place so that he could attend him as much as he could.

Some nights, he kept awake beside the bed. But the cancer did spread quickly, and Mr. Chung lost his voice. The five-foot-three-inch tall man was reduced to 85 pounds. He lost 25 pounds to the rapidly spreading cancer.

Following her son's advice, Young Oak kept talking to her husband who could not speak, as he lay in a hospital bed. She repeatedly told him how grateful she was for his help for her family.   She also whispered to him the memories of the early years on the plantation. Whether he was listening or not, she kept reliving for him the funny as well as sad episodes.

On July 20, 1952, Mr. Chung passed away. His wife and six children were by his side, attending him during the last moments of his life. One of the first Korean immi-grants in Hawaii rested in sleep in the country where he had rooted and branched. Like many of his fellow country-men, he used to say that "any place one falls in love with becomes one's hometown." His bitterness over the loss of the political independence of Korea faded away in his con-cern about meeting the needs of the growing family. He kept the Korean passport issued in 1904. He rejected any suggestion to obtain a Japanese passport for travel. He did not see himself bowing to Japanese officials as a Japanese subject. He loved Hawaii. He never wished to travel out-side the Hawaiian islands for 50 years, not even to return to Korea.

At the graveside of her husband, Mrs. Chung felt a sudden void in her life. The man she always called "father" lay in silence. From the moment she had received his pic-ture until the moment he succumbed to the throat cancer, he was dominant in her life. The stoic old soldier didn't show affection to his young wife, but he cared deeply for the woman he had picked to marry. He frequently told his sons to look after their mother after he was gone. He knew his wife would have to live as a widow for many years.

At his grave, Young Oak cried, "Father, father, you worked so hard to help my parents and our six children. You fed my family when they had no money to buy food. I will never forget your generosity until I die. You rest in peace." Then she passed out.   When she regained consciousness, Mrs. Chung refused to leave the cemetery until the burial was over.

His body is resting at the Nuannu cemetery. He died with the assurance that his wife would stay next to him when her time comes. As they were together in this world, they will stay together in death.

Moments of Indignation

During the 34 years of their marriage, only on two occasions did Mr. Chung lay hands on his wife out of indignation.   The first incident happened in the church of which they were members.   There was a dispute over Reverend Jang Boong who had been transferred from Shanghai. Because he was critical of some of the things Dr. Rhee, the founder of the Hawaii Korean Church had done, those members who were extremely loyal to Dr. Rhee insisted that the pastor had to be dismissed.   The support for Dr. Rhee Syngman among the Comrade Society members was such that if someone failed to mention Dr. Rhee's name in his public prayer, that member would be considered disloyal. Others in the same congregation argued that the pastor shouldn't be dismissed. After many heated debates, the congregation decided to vote on the future of their pastor.

It was an open vote using ballots. As the vote of each ballot was counted, it turned out that Mr. Chung voted in favor of dismissal and his wife against it. When he heard of his wife's 'nay' vote, he strode to her and slapped her hard across her face. In anger, he shouted at his wife, "Husband and wife should be one mind and one body, but you voted against your husband's wish. You know where I stand on this issue. Don't you know that a divided family is headed for ruin?"

The other church members separated Mr. Chung from his wife, whose face was badly swollen. Some chided Mr. Chung for hitting his wife in such a manner.

Young Oak calmly responded to her husband, "Everyone has the right to vote according to conscience. Otherwise there is no need to take a vote to resolve an issue. This is America. I simply exercised my own religious freedom." She continued, "If we hire and dismiss a servant of God according to political considerations, it is improper. We have to differentiate between religious principle and political expedience." When Young Oak finished the statement, the church members on both sides of the issue applauded her.

To save her husband's face in this embarrassing situation, Young Oak endorsed his action. "My husband did what he did to me because he loves me and our family. I have no doubt about it. Therefore, I am not angry at my husband."

Both Mr. Chung's display of anger and his wife's firm stand for belief surprised many. Later Mr. Chung proved to be right on the issue. The pastor had to be dismissed for improper conduct.

The other time Mr. Chung slapped his wife concerned his brother-in-law. He had heard that his wife's brother in Japan had married the wife of a fellow plantation worker.

After three years of unhappy married life, the woman had left her husband under the pretext that she would go to Korea for infertility treatment. Instead, she went to Japan and told Young Oak's brother that she had been in America and had received a college education. She said she had returned to Japan to assist the Korean students' independence movement. The woman had known of Young Oak's brother from Young Oak who had been fond of telling others about her brother's study in Japan. As they worked closely in Japan, they became more than comrades. Eventually, the two crossed the line and were married.

When the news reached Hawaii, someone reported it to Mr. Chung. "Mr. Chung, I know you have sent a lot of money to support your wife's family, especially her brother in Japan. But look at what your money did to him. He snatched your fellow worker's wife."

Mr. Chung was furious. As soon as he came home, he threw his lunch box on the floor and slapped his wife mercilessly. At first, she didn't know why her husband was being so rude to her.   "You must carry bad blood in your vein like your brother," he blurted out. "I can't believe I have supported a wife-snatcher with my hard-earned money. You know that I earned the money by back-breaking plantation labor. I can tell you that you married me, not because you loved me but because you wanted to help your parents and siblings. But what is the result of my help? How in the world can a man marry someone else's wife?" He was full of disappointment and disbelief. He even suspected that his wife was a part of the conspiracy.

The shameful news came to Young Oak unexpectedly. She didn't know a thing about the woman's intent. She was speechless over her brother's shameful act. So she slipped away and stayed at her friend's house until late that night. She was so afraid of her husband that she sneaked back into the house through a window and slept on the floor.

Young Oak had never seen her husband so indignant. He didn't go to work the next day. This scared Young Oak very much because he had never missed work for personal reasons. Only after the husband of the betrayed woman came to assure Mr. Chung that Mrs. Chung had nothing to do with his wife's infidelity did he return to normal. His friend even scolded Mr. Chung for treating his innocent young wife roughly.

That was the end of Mr. Chung's support of his wife's brother. For almost ten years, Young Oak didn't hear from her brother.

Surprises

Young Oak was really surprised when she heard from other Korean women of some almost unbelievable episodes involving her husband. It was an unexpected discovery of another side to her husband.

At the end of each day, the plantation workers showered together in the company shower room. To relieve the monotony and boredom of farm labor, they teased each other a lot about almost anything. Everyone was vulnerable in the public shower room when they were exposed.

One day the Korean workers teased Mr. Chung that they were amazed at his procreative power since he had produced as many as six boys in spite of his small body and reproductive organ. Such a joke was not confined to shower room teasing. Apparently the men shared the joke with their wives.

One Saturday, which was a pay day, Mr. Chung stopped by to chat with a friend. Instead, he was met by a roomful of women. They demanded Mr. Chung prove that he actually fathered the six boys. In a jolly mood, Mr. Chung turned around and pulled down his trousers. It caught everyone in the room by surprise. None of them imagined such a bold act coming from the stoic Mr. Chung. It was totally uncharacteristic of the strict man. He did, however, vindicate his wife's fidelity and, at the same time, his manliness.

Taking advantage of Mr. Chung's jolly mood, Hanna Cho took him outside and poured water over him by holding a water hose over his head. In a ceremonious tone Hanna said, "Mr. Chung, you have to wash off old-fashioned Korean ideas and attitudes. You must always remember that you live in 20th-century America. From now on act like someone living in America, not in Korea." Mr. Chung took the jocular ceremony in a light spirit.

A few days later, the women visited Young Oak and told her in detail what Mr. Chung did and what they did to him. They admonished Young Oak rather seriously. "You are the one who has kept Mr. Chung so old-fashioned. You treat your old husband with too much respect. You are foolish. Demand him to treat you with affection, otherwise, threaten him with divorce. We cannot believe that your husband did not touch your stomach even once when you were pregnant with his six babies. Even by the old Korean standard, he is too strict and bland."

But Young Oak felt that it would be almost as impossible to change her attitude toward her husband as to change her husband. To her he was always a father figure, not a husband.

Another time Mr. Chung surprised others was at a time of mourning. There was an old Korean lady who died at her son's house in Honolulu. Many Koreans visited the family, and some stayed with the family at nights according to the Korean custom. Some got the idea that Mr. Chung was about the same size and shape as Elizabeth Chun, who had died. So they made him put on some of the woman's clothes that were familiar to many. Then they had him sit in the middle of the living room with his head facing the floor. The camouflaged Mr. Chung looked just like the dead woman. The practical joke was to change the sad mood of the bereaved family and visitors.

As the visitors entered the room, they screamed at the sitting figure of the dead woman. Momentarily, they thought that they were seeing the ghost of Elizabeth Chun. It was awfully hard not to believe that the sitting figure was someone else. Later they were doubly shocked when they discovered that the figure was none other than Mr. Chung Bong Woon, the least likely person to do such a practical joke.

When the Korean visitors broke into noisy laughter, the puzzled neighbors of other nationalities came to discover what was happening in the house of mourning.

Adjustment

Mr. Chung used to playfully call his wife a "$1,000 picture bride," meaning that he had sent about that amount to her home during their engagement. Even after marriage, he sent more money to help his wife's family.

Although he was not an affectionate husband and father, he at least provided security for his wife and children. He never treated himself with leisure and comfort until he was in his 70's but kept working as if born just to work. He understood the word "idleness" conceptually but never experienced it. Besides his regular employment, he made extra money wholesaling fruits and vegetables in odd hours. The stability of his family life might be attributed to the economic security he had maintained through hard work.

In later years, whenever Young Oak expressed an opinion different from her husband's, he would remind his wife of the early years. "I have raised you all these years. Now you dare to have your own ideas." Young Oak was troubled by such treatment, but she did not want to challenge the authority of her husband. She conditioned herself to respect and obey him without question. Furthermore, she valued the peace of the family as far more important than anything in her own life.

Young Oak was often mistaken for Mr. Chung's daughter by strangers in a new neighborhood. They would say to Young Oak, "I see your father in the house. Where is your husband?"

Young Oak was only 51 when she became a widow. Not long after her husband's death, she decided to have her hair cut. For the first time in her life she had a hairdresser curl her hair. Since Mr. Chung had ordered his wife not to accept the American short-cut hairstyle, she had no choice but to obey him. Slowly, Young Oak learned to make decisions without worrying about her husband's opinion or criticism.

9

THE LADY V.I.P.

When Mrs. Chung and the members of the Comrade Society heard the news that Dr. Rhee Syngman had been elected the first president of the Republic of Korea in 1948, they all were elated. After loyally supporting their leader for almost 30 years, they finally saw him as the founding leader of the new republic. Many felt that their mission for the homeland had been accomplished.

In 1949 the Korean government invited the former supporters of its president to the first anniversary of Dr. Rhee's inauguration. The president made a special request to include only those above 70 years of age. The president himself was 74, and he felt that the old comrades in Hawaii should see the independent Korea and its new government. He knew that independence from Japanese colonial rule had been the life-long dream and mission of many overseas Koreans.

Through the arrangements of Mr. Hong Chan, a prominent figure in the Korean film industry and a staunch supporter of the president, a charter plane was sent to Hawaii. The Hawaii Korean delegates consisted of 46 older Comrade Society members, a physician, a nurse, and Mrs. Chung Young Oak representing the Hawaii Korean Church. Mrs. Chung was only 47.

Young Oak's second visit to Korea was far more glorious and meaningful than her first one in 1935. This time she came as a special guest of the president. She could not hide her excitement. Both of her dreams had finally come true. First, her family had become wealthy and reputable, with her brothers and sisters all doing well in their chosen professions. Secondly, Korea had become an independent nation under the leadership of Dr. Rhee Syngman whom she had supported all these years.

The Hawaiian delegates were treated like returning war heroes from a victorious foreign expedition. Everywhere they visited, they were met with welcoming placards and speeches. They were given credit for the success of the independence movement through their sacrificial support for the first president and his movement. Every welcoming speaker made a reference to the patriotic support of the Hawaiian Koreans. Many of the delegates were emotionally overwhelmed as they were reminded of the long years of personal struggle in Hawaii.

At one welcoming rally, the speaker gave a six-foot long welcoming-speech script to Young Oak. It read:

> Every March the swallows visit the homeland from the South and make nests for their summer stay. Every July, Kyunwoo and Jikyu cross the milky way to meet on the bridge hastily made of the magpie heads. But you delegates left the homeland behind and spent so many years in a strange land where the language and customs are very different. You have built your new life with hard physical labor for over fifty years and finally established a proud Korean community there. We are so moved and touched by the homecoming of the thirty-three fathers and thirteen sisters. You were so young when you left

the homeland, and now you have returned with gray hairs and wrinkles.

How vividly do you remember when you left Korea decades ago? Perhaps you ladies were wearing long skirts and you gentlemen were still carrying the top-notch. The Sun always rises in the east and sets in the west. The spring flowers are always red and the autumn moon is bright. However, in the midst of ever-changing history, our country became the victim of oppression. Our bodies were chained and our mouths were gagged for thirty-six years. During this time, many Koreans were martyred at home and abroad, and we went through the two terrible World Wars. Korea became the beneficiary of the decisive, humiliating defeat of Japan at the end of the Second World War. The red blood of the martyred patriots turned into the national flower of hibiscus.

As the result of their sacrifices, we are able to celebrate the Korean Independence Day on August fifteenth. When the Declaration of Independence was echoed at home and abroad, the Hawaii-Koreans generously supported the Korean Provisional Government established in Sanghai with their hard-earned money. Moreover, you took care of many exiled leaders and sometimes you extended your helping hands to the needs of home. The Heaven was deeply moved by such unselfish supports and it granted us the independence. Yet our fatherland is still divided.

We free people really welcome the Hawaii delegates to the celebration of the independence of our homeland. There are one hundred people but only one mind. Even if there are one hundred minds, we are united for one purpose. Whenever we climb a tree, we remember its roots and when we drink water, we remember its origin. We pray that as you end the journey of thorny path without a country, you may continue your support for the reconstruction of our country with pride and determination. May God be with each of you forty-six delegates for many years to come.

The 4288th Year of Korea Origin, October 24th
The Joint Welcoming Rally of Korean Women Associations, Choi Eun-hi

The Hawaiian delegates met their old leader in the presidential office. It was an emotional but joyful reunion. After shaking hands and embracing his old comrades, the president spoke to the delegates.

"Without your support and sacrifice, I would not have been in this position today. I am really grateful for your help during my stay in Hawaii. But we all did only what we had to do as Koreans."

Some of the delegates became choked with tears.

The old delegates told the president that this might be the last time they would see their old friend and walk on the soil of their free motherland. They knew their old age and the enormous distance would not permit a second visit to Korea. Many proudly told the president that finally they could die with their eyes closed.

Some brought chocolates to the president, who loved that Hawaiian delicacy. Others gave him money, an old habit during the independence movement in Hawaii.

When the delegates bid farewell to the president, some of them were hurt. Somehow the president sent away the old comrades without serving a dinner. The former plantation workers anticipated the honor of having a dinner with him. After all, they were the guests of the president. They speculated that either the new government was too poor to treat the delegates or the government ignored them. During their five-day stay, the old delegates had a hard time. The food and accommodations were not up to their expectations.

The return trip by the same plane was an anticlimax. Flying against the trade winds, the plane behaved like a toy plane in a stormy sky. The plane was mercilessly rocked and tossed by the wind. It was too much trauma for the old delegates to take. When the plane finally managed to land in Honolulu, two were taken straight to the Queen's Hospital from which they did not leave alive.

One by one, the old delegates died almost every year. But no one regretted the unforgettable trip to Korea. Their last dream had come true.

At The Request Of the First Lady

The first lady, Mrs. Francesca Rhee, requested Mrs. Chung to lead a campaign in Korea to discourage the desire among highly educated Korean women to go to America. The first lady was quite disturbed that well-educated Koreans were more interested in going overseas for personal success than taking part in rebuilding their new country.

The first lady chose Mrs. Chung for the job for a number of reasons. By this time, she could easily afford the travel and personal expense without any government help. With almost unrestricted financial support from her well-to-do children in Hawaii, she could stay in the best hotel in Seoul, the Bando Hotel, for weeks if necessary.

Secondly, she had gone through the hardship of American life herself. The former picture bride could share with her audience the first-hand experience of living on the sugar plantations and raising six boys. The first lady figured that such a powerful personal testimony might discourage the aspiring Korean women.

Thirdly, the first lady knew the unquestionable patriotism of Mrs. Chung, which she had demonstrated in her support of Dr. Rhee and his independence movement.

Finally, she was an enthusiastic public speaker, easily moving the minds of her audience. In spite of only a few years of elementary education, her speech was eloquent. Her long-time association with leading Korean political figures had raised her ears.

Mrs. Chung accepted the challenge if it would help in curbing the female brain drain. In order to travel around the country, she brought in a new Chrysler for which she paid 3,000 dollars at the customs office. She was tempted to contact the president's office so as to avoid paying the excessive customs fee. She needed the car for the campaign requested by the president's wife. But she decided to abide by the law regardless of the circumstances.

The president's office arranged her speaking schedule. At school and after school, she spoke passionately for the rebuilding of the country and appealed to her female audience to take part in this historic mission. At the same time, she tried to portray America as not so rosy a paradise as the girls imagined. She had plenty of examples of painful experiences in America.

One day, she went to one of the best girl's high schools in Korea. In the middle of her speech in the school yard, girls passed out here and there. Mrs. Chung could not figure out why the girls were suddenly dropping. Later the teachers told her that the girls could not stand the summer heat because they were so weak from malnutrition. According to the teachers, it was a common occurrence for some girls to skip both breakfast and lunch. Mrs. Chung thought that the campaign was irrelevant to many who were struggling just to survive in their own country. So she decided to end her campaign.

Building a Church in Seoul

Having the founder of the Hawaii Korean Church as the president, some church members in Hawaii proposed building a branch church in Seoul. They thought that the branch church of the Hawaii Korean Church would serve as a constant reminder of the president's patriotic spirit and work in Hawaii. Furthermore, they wanted to extend the legacy of the overseas Korean Christian independence movement to the homeland.

Reverend Lee Jong Kwan was one such enthusiast. He had served the Koreans in Hawaii for many years. More than once, he was elected the president of the Korean National Association of Hawaii. In spite of his old age, 85, he volunteered for the task. He thought that this would be his last project for the people and the country he loved so much.

Knowing his physical and social limits, Reverend Lee asked Mrs. Chung to assist him in the project. He knew well that Mrs. Chung had money, time, connections, and, above all, enthusiasm. Mrs. Chung could not turn down the appeal of the old minister, and she accepted the challenge.

As soon as the two arrived in Korea, they visited the president for his help. Reverend Lee explained the purpose of the project to his old friend. "Mr. President, I knew all along you would be president someday. Hearty congratulations. I came to Korea to build a branch church of the Hawaii Korean Church. Since it was founded by none other than you, we think such a project is very significant and timely. I would very much appreciate it if you would kindly see to it that the necessary assistance be arranged for the worthy project."

The president responded to the proposal without much thought. "Reverend Lee, I think you are too old to have your hands on such a project. Why don't you go back to Hawaii and enjoy the rest of your life in peace. I am sorry to say this, but the poor Korean government doesn't have money for such a project. Unless you find money elsewhere, you had better give up the project." Obviously, the president was indifferent to the proposal and even annoyed by the request.

"Dr. Rhee, I never imagined you would respond this way. What makes you think that I, Lee Jong Kwan, cannot build a church in the motherland which has become independent?"

The furious Reverend Lee walked out of the president's office without saying a word to him. It was the last meeting of the two old comrades, and it had ended in a chilly confrontation. Mrs. Chung felt awkward being caught between the two old veterans of the independence movement.

Quite disappointed but not giving up, the old minister asked Mrs. Chung to do her best for the project. But building a sizable church in the capital without ready money was not an easy task at all. The high hope of having the president's support for the project quickly evaporated, so Young Oak seriously thought of returning to Hawaii.

One day while she was eating at a restaurant, she noticed a small boy living on the change handed to him by customers for putting loose shoes in order in the entrance hall. A uniformed soldier kicked the boy because he was slow in bringing the soldier's shoes. The boy fell to the ground a few feet away and cried hysterically. Young Oak was furious. She yelled at others in the restaurant to catch the rude soldier, but he managed to flee the scene. Young Oak said loudly, "Isn't a soldier's duty to protect his countrymen? What a barbaric act. I am going to see that the soldier is arrested and punished severely." Then she asked the restaurant manager to take the little boy to a hospital for examination. She said she would take care of the hospital bill.

In the same restaurant, there was a woman soldier who had been watching Young Oak. The woman soldier knew that the sophisticated-looking lady was a powerful woman with some high connections. The way the lady spoke and conducted herself unmistakably conveyed such a message.

Before leaving the restaurant, the woman soldier apologized to Mrs. Chung for the misconduct of the man. Then she asked for Mrs. Chung's address and telephone number. In the course of the conversation, the woman soldier found out that the lady was staying at the Bando Hotel and that she was close to President Rhee and his wife.

The next morning Mrs. Chung was sent for by the four-star general Lee Hyung Keun. General Lee politely apologized for the soldier's rudeness in the restaurant.

Mrs. Chung grabbed the opportunity to tell him why she was in the country and what her problems were. Right there, General Lee summoned other generals, including those in charge of the Army Corp of Engineers and treasury. He told his staff generals to assist Mrs. Chung as much as they could. As a result of the meeting, the army would provide building material and labor. But she still had to obtain a piece of property for the church building project.

She finally found a site on a rocky hill, not far from the president's residence. It couldn't be better. The affluent residents at the bottom of the hill, however, objected to a church being built. They were concerned about noise, traffic, and especially flood during the summer rainy season. The residents included Mr. Hu Jung (the mayor of Seoul) and Mr. Yoon Bo Sun (former mayor of Seoul, assembly man, and later president), to name a few. With powerful persuasion and lobbying, Young Oak got a building permit from the city.

By this time, she was well recognized by top government officials who had seen the lady from Hawaii always sitting close to the president on many public occasions. She seemed to have free access to the president and the first lady. Her appearance on television, radio, and in print made her well known. Using her prestige and influence, she was selling hard the idea of building a church as a monument of the president's life-long struggle for Korean independence.

The army generals and high-ranking government officials seemed to recognize the value of the project. In the course of her negotiations, she met three four-star army generals. They were Generals Lee Hyung Keun, Baik Sun Yup, and Jung Il Kwon. With the help of the Army Corp of Engineers, the branch of the Hawaii Korean Church was finally completed.

Mrs. Chung stayed at the expensive Bando Hotel for months over the three year period during which the church was being built. She didn't get a single penny from anyone for the project. Her children covered all of their mother's expenses. They never asked questions about how their money was spent for they absolutely trusted that their mother was doing something worthwhile for the motherland.

Reverend Lee died three days after the completion of the church. The president heard of the completion of the project when the death of his old friend was reported in the newspapers. As they were going to bury the body of the minister near the church, the president ordered that his friend be buried in a cemetery on the outskirt of the capital city.

Marriage Proposals

Since her husband's death in 1952, Young Oak's friends in Honolulu and Seoul had suggested that she remarry. Even her own children sincerely hoped that their mother would find a man to her liking. Every time their mother returned from a trip to Korea, they were anxious to know if she would announce good news regarding marriage. Knowing that their father was much older and more old-fashioned than their mother, they really wanted to see her enjoy the second half of her life with the right man. By this time money was at her disposal.

For years Mrs. Chung got acquainted with the Korean medical doctors who came to Honolulu for medical training. During one of her stays in Korea, Mrs. Chung was introduced to a widower physician through her old acquaintances.

They told her that he was a successful surgeon practicing in Pusan. So Young Oak was interested in him and invited the surgeon to a dinner at the Bando Hotel. After the dinner, her guest offered to sing a song for the happy occasion. The influence of alcohol made him somewhat imprudent, and he acted as if he were in a bar with a kisaeng (geisha). This offended Young Oak. Later he apologized for his inappropriate manner, but she had lost interest.

One of the impressive men Young Oak got acquainted with during her frequent visits to the capital city was Mr. Kim Hong Il, who was the ambassador to the Republic of China (Taiwan). He was a well-built, handsome man who had lost his wife. Whenever the two happened to visit Seoul at the same time, they enjoyed each other's company as old friends. Young Oak respected the man for his love for the country.

Mr. Kim had a colorful military career during the days of the Independence Movement in China. He had been appointed a commander of both the Korean and Chinese armies at various levels. His troops had engaged in the anti-Japanese combats in Manchuria. During the Korean war, the general had been the commander of the First Army Corps. He had retired from the Korean Army in 1954. In the same year, he had been appointed an ambassador to the Republic of China.

One day the ambassador invited Young Oak to visit him in Taipei, and he sent a round-trip plane ticket. Young Oak read the invitation as a signal for a marriage proposal. In spite of her tight schedule, she accepted the invitation and flew to Taipei. When she arrived in the Korean embassy, she saw that the ambassador was living in quite pitiful quarters. Being a widower, Ambassador Kim had a housemaid, a small Chinese girl. To the affluent lady from Hawaii, the scene was almost shocking. The kitchen at the ambassador's residence reminded her of the outdoor kitchen at the plantation house. For the first time, she saw with her own eyes the real official poverty of the poor country behind the glorious title.

As usual, their conversation began with politics. The two patriots hotly debated the legitimacy of Dr. Rhee's running for a fourth term. Mrs. Chung objected to his running for a fourth time in the face of strong opposition from the Korean people, let alone the outright unconstitutionality of serving a fourth term.

But the president's appointee insisted that Dr. Rhee was the only qualified leader to rule the country. She had heard the same argument time and again, and Young Oak thought that the ambassador had been blinded by his own political interest.

Sensing the ambassador's ambiguous attitudes toward his guest, Young Oak asked a pointed question the next day. "Mr. Ambassador, aren't you tired of the impoverished politician's life? I think you have done more than your share of sacrifice for the country. I think you deserve a comfortable life in your old age. Have you ever thought about going to Hawaii and enjoying the leisurely American life?"

Looking straight at his guest, Ambassador Kim raised his voice, "A frog should live in his pond. Likewise a man should live according to his lot. An old man like me, what would I do in Hawaii? I am destined to be a politician until I die."

Young Oak instantly figured out that the ambassador would not be interested in going to America. At the same time, she could not imagine herself living far away from her six sons and their families. The last thing she would trade for anything in the world would be closeness to her six sons. Furthermore, she thought that she could not adjust to the meager life of the average Korean family. Every time she visited Korea, she stayed only at the Bando Hotel and drank and ate only the hotel food. She did not risk drinking and eating outside the hotel after eating at countryside restaurants and getting two terrible stomachaches that made her sick for days. She was uneasy about the encounter with the old friend, so she felt relieved when she flew out of the Taipei airport.

In Touch with the Inner Circle

Young Oak's association with Korean government officials was not limited just to those of the ruling party. When Vice-president Jang Myun (the leader of the opposition party) was wounded by an assassin's bullet in 1956, she visited him at the hospital. Her visit surprised the vice-president.

"I did not expect to see the right hand of President Rhee. So why are you visiting me?"

"An old friend is not supposed to discern who is on my side or who is on my enemy's side now. I simply want to express my sympathy. I sincerely wish you a quick recovery."

One day Mrs. Chung visited the man second in power in Korea. It was Mr. Lee Key Boong, the Speaker of the Korean National Assembly. The man became very influential when he managed to have the childless president adopt his own son, Lee Kang Suk. Speaker Lee was considered by many the successor of President Rhee.

As she was entering the office of the Assembly Speaker one day, she saw Mr. Lee ignoring her entrance. Pointing her finger at the speaker she commanded in English, "Mr. Lee, you get up from your seat. Don't you recognize my entrance?"

The embarrassed speaker slowly stood up with a forced smile. "Sister Chung, I did not know you were coming in. I am sorry for the discourtesy."

Young Oak's last meeting with the president in his official residence was less than cordial. Having kept her ears to the ground, Young Oak knew well the sentiment of the Korean people toward their president and government. But the president, tightly surrounded by loyal supporters was out of touch with the people. His Austrian wife didn't help him in this regard. Young Oak made an appeal to the insulated president.

"Mr. President, please do not run for the fourth term. The tide of the people's opinion is definitely against you."

The president, noticeably annoyed, snapped, "Mrs. Chung, where did you hear such an unfounded story? You must have been influenced by some anti-government elements. Don't you dare tell me what I should and should not do."

"OK, Mr. President," she responded.

As she was leaving the president's office, the first lady called Young Oak in.

"Mrs. Chung, whenever you see the president, he gets quite disturbed. Therefore I ask you not to see him again."

Young Oak loved the president, but that did not make her blind and deaf about the political situation of the country.

When the president won the election in March 1960 through fraud and corruption, the country exploded. Thousands of high school and college students poured into the streets to protest the dictatorial government. It was a bloody confrontation between the armed police and students. Many protesting students were felled like early spring flowers by police bullets, but the students were determined to overthrow Rhee's regime at all costs.

The beginning of the end of Rhee's regime was set when the president's adopted son carried out family suicide. Sensing the irreversible political tide and its grave consequence to his family, he shot his real parents and siblings. Then he killed himself.

The tragic news shocked the president. After 195 lives of young students and civilians and over 6,000 injuries, President Rhee could not withstand the political pressures anymore. On April 28, he announced his resignation from the presidency of over 10 years.

Many recited the Korean maxim, "No red flower lasts for ten days and no dictatorial regime lasts for ten years."

When Young Oak heard of the overthrow of the regime, she was sad. But she had known it was coming. The end of Dr. Rhee's power was the end of Young Oak's contact with the inner circle of Korean government.

However, the subsequent Korean rulers, Presidents Park Chung Hee and Chun Doo Whan, did not forget to recognize the life-long patriot. When they stopped over in Honolulu during their state visits to America, the Honolulu consulate office included the woman's name on the official guest list. The young presidents loved to hear her story about old Korean politics in Hawaii. But Young Oak never developed a personal relationship with the new inner circle of government. In spite of their suggestions to visit them in Seoul, Young Oak never set foot in the official residence of the new presidents. She felt that she belonged to the old guard.

Encounter with President Johnson

Although she had no tie with an American politician, she had concern for the political well-being of her adoptive country. She had felt sorrow as deep as any other American citizen when President Roosevelt died in the middle of the Second World War. To win the war, she was willing to send her children for military service.

When President Johnson was to have a major operation, Young Oak prayed for the success of the surgery. One night she had a dream. In it she saw the healthy-looking president repairing a road with a shovel. The president kept showing his unique big smile. This dream assured her that the president would recover fully.

She wrote a letter in Korean and mailed it to the White House. In the letter to the president, she described her dream in detail and assured him of a successful recovery from the operation.

One day the Korean Consulate General of Honolulu informed Mrs. Chung of receiving a letter to her from the White House. In the letter, the president thanked her for her prayer and thoughtfulness. She met President Johnson at the Korean Consulate General of Honolulu when he stopped on his way to visit Korea in 1967. She never forgets the moment of shaking hands with the president.

The arrival of Hawaiian Korean delegates in 1949 (above) and
Mrs. Chung welcomed by her brother at the airport

Beside the statue of Dr. Rhee Syngman (above)
Around President Rhee Syngman (below)

Commendation she recieved from the president. It reads: "Commendment.
Chung Young Oak. This is to acknowledge the meritous service toward the
overseas Korean independence movement. March first of the fifth year of the
Republic of Korea. President Rhee Syngman. Republic of Korea" (above). Young
Oak with Mr. Lee Key Boong, Speaker of the Korean National Assembly (below).

With General Baek Sun Yup and Ambassador to Japan, Mr.
Chung Kyung Whan (above)
and General Lee Hyung Ken (below)

The statue of Dr. Rhee Syngman erected on the grounds of the
Hawaii Korean Christian Church on the 40th anniversary of Korean
independence (above) and Mrs. Chung before the corner stone of the
Seoul branch of the Hawaii Korean Christian Church (below)

10

DEATH OF A
PRESIDENT

The day Dr. Rhee and his wife, Francesca, were on their way to exile in Hawaii found Young Oak really heart-broken. She was bitter about the turn of events. The twists of the politician's fate were beyond her comprehension.

The life-long patriot began his political life in exile in the United States more than half a century before, and he seemed to end it with a second exile. She thought that the first exile was something to be proud of. But this time the former president was fleeing the country for which he had spent all his years and energy. He was running away from the people who used to call him a founding father.

Young Oak went to the airport to greet the former president. At the airport she met some of her old comrades, loyal supporters of Dr. Rhee's political movement. They also expressed a great deal of disappointment about the return of their leader.

The eighty-five-year-old president looked tired and drained as he descended from the plane. When he set foot on the ground, he tried to stand erect with the dignity of a former president. But the old man had a hard time walking without the help of his wife and accompanying guards.

The former president was pleased to see the sizable crowd. Some of his supporters wiped away tears as they saw the pitiful return to exile of the rejected president.

He shook hands with each in the welcoming party. When he came to Young Oak, she could not help but saying what she felt about him.

"Dr. Rhee, you should not have left Korea no matter how adverse the situation was." It was a blunt greeting.

"You are right, Mrs. Chung, but Francesca made this arrangement through the U.S. Embassy. I had no choice but to comply with the U.S. government request." The president sounded helpless.

After the President stepped down from his office, the reaction of the people at home troubled Dr. Rhee's supporters in Hawaii, including Young Oak.

On the TV screen, they saw angry citizens and students in Seoul trample on official portraits of Dr. Rhee they had removed from the walls of school classrooms and public buildings. Some burned the portraits in the streets while the crowd cheered. Others removed Dr. Rhee's statues and dragged them through the streets of the capital city. The people in the streets spat at the statues and kicked them while cursing.

To Hawaiian Koreans, their fellow Koreans at home seemed to have forgotten what he had done for his country all these years. They felt that if they had known the personal sacrifice Dr. Rhee had endured for the independence of Korea, they would not have done such an ungrateful, shameful thing. Young Oak, who traveled frequently to Korea and kept up with the political situation there, felt that the mob actions were excessive. Some of Dr. Rhee's supporters felt that their involvement in the Korean Independence Movement had been futile.

Even in exile, the former president could not forget the country he loved so much. His one remaining wish was to die in the country of his ancestry and be buried there. The many years of his residence in America did not change the last wish of every Korean man: to die at the place of his birth.

On many occasions, the former president quoted the expression, "Even old tigers return to their caves to take the last breath there before they die."

Every Sunday he would come to the Hawaii Korean Church and take the very front seat with his wife. In spite of his effort to be cheerful, the people could not help but detect sadness in his countenance.

His relentless request for return was finally granted by the military government of President Park Chung Hee. This made the old man happy because his last wish was finally coming true. One day while busily preparing for his return, the former president received a cable from the Korean government: "the grant of your return has been reversed." There was no explanation as to why the military government had cancelled the earlier decision.

Still holding the cable in his right hand and trembling violently, the former president screamed, "Ah!" That momentary shock locked his fists, and he lost his mind. Soon after he was hospitalized, the doctors had to use instruments to unfold his fingers. They discovered that his locked fingers had caused severe blisters in his palms.

Young Oak frequently visited Dr. Rhee at the hospital. She made sure that the old couple had their needs taken care of. One day, Francesca told Young Oak that Dr. Rhee had affectionately called her 'booin' (equivalent to 'wife'). Francesca felt that her husband was finally accepting her as the wife of a Korean man. Young Oak who was close to the couple knew the significance of such an affectionate expression from the former president. Young Oak was glad that the couple were getting closer to each other in this time of difficulty.

Francesca also told Young Oak that Dr. Rhee kept chanting old Korean poems in his hospital bed. It was a habit he had developed during the years of his presidency. Nobody knew what poems he was chanting in the early morning hours. Perhaps they spoke of the vanity of life.

On July 19, 1965, the old patriot died, 90 years old, in the land in which he had been twice exiled. He turned out to be less fortunate than the tiger he used to compare himself to. His dream of freedom for his country was achieved, but not his simple wish of dying in his native land.

Apparently the Korean government was not afraid of the dead tiger, and his last wish was posthumously granted. The body of the president was flown to Seoul by a special U.S. Air Force transport plane.

This was the second time the freedom-fighter crossed the Pacific Ocean in a coffin. Not many knew Dr. Rhee smuggled himself in a luxury coffin to Shanghai to avoid Japanese inspection during the stopovers at the Japanese harbors. His American supporter, the operator of Borthwick Mortuary in Honolulu, designed a special coffin for ventilation and food supply.

Young Oak was asked by the Korean government to accompany his body, but she refused to go with the dead president. She was bitter about the government that had treated the former president with disrespect.

President Park Chung Hee declared a "people's funeral" for the late president. It was the second highest honor accorded to a prominent national figure in Korea. When the car carrying the body of the former president slowly made its way through the capital city, approximately 300,000 Seoul citizens lined the streets to pay their last homage to the old patriot. Many citizens bid farewell with tears.

Recollections

Young Oak felt a big void in her life. No one had had a greater impact upon her life than Dr. Rhee. He was the one who had stirred her political passion. She really respected the imposing figure who showed what it meant to be a patriot.

Dr. Rhee gave his followers a focus for their lives. In the Independence movement, Young Oak found something larger than the mundane concerns of her own family. Her active involvement in the movement kept her immigrant life on the plantation from the doldrums. She experienced a kind of transcendence as she identified with the causes of the Korean community in Hawaii. The picture bride from a humble background became a part of a great historical movement.

From her first year in Hawaii to the last moment of Dr. Rhee's life, she had supported the patriot from the bottom of her heart. The death of Dr. Rhee left a vacuum in Young Oak's life.

Young Oak's relationship with Dr. Rhee was a close one, more than just leader to follower. Personal concerns were mutually expressed. He used to say to his faithful supporter, "Mrs. Chung, I am really thankful for your diligent support for the cause of Korean independence. I know life on the plantation with the old husband and the six boys is hard for you. But don't let discouragement take over. Endure the hardships with patience and hope. Someday you will be greatly rewarded."

Dr. Rhee took note of Mrs. Chung's positive outlook and broad-mindedness, unusual traits among Korean women. When there were disputes among the factions in the Hawaii Korean community, sometimes she volunteered for the role of mediation. For such a role, she was respected by leadership on both sides. Also her active involvement in church work had impressed many.

Dr. Rhee's wife, Francesca, was also grateful to Young Oak for helping the couple many times during their stay in Hawaii.

Dr. Rhee had lived alone for almost thirty years since he had come to America in 1904. The handsome old bachelor with a Ph.D. from Princeton University became the object of respect and inspiration among Koreans. Furthermore, his undivided devotion to the cause of Korean independence touched many of his supporters and foes alike. He ended his lonely bachelor's life when he met an Austrian woman. Through the introduction of an American friend in Washington, D.C., Dr. Rhee met Miss Francesca Donner. This daughter of an Austrian businessman was an enthusiastic fan of the exiled Korean leader. She followed him almost everywhere he went to hear his political speeches and public debates on the subject of Korean independence. Of course, she was more than a fan. She wanted to marry the prominent Korean in exile.

As the Korean saying goes, "There is no tree that doesn't fall after ten ax choppings." Dr. Rhee fell in love with her, and they were married in New York in 1934. It was his second marriage.

His first marriage hadn't lasted long. First, the marriage was arranged by his parents according to age-old Korean tradition. However, the bright, restless young man was too Western to be content. Moreover, his prolonged imprisonment in Korea and his extended stay in America put his Korean wife in an unfortunate position. They were divorced, and Dr. Rhee took care of his only son from the first marriage who died at an early age in the States.

The news of Dr. Rhee's marriage to Francesca Donner sent waves of shock through the members of the Comrade Society. Many Korean supporters were disappointed by their leader's interracial marriage. Some were even angry at their leader who was considered to have betrayed Korean identity. For years Dr. Rhee kept telling his followers that the Korean people in America should learn the mother tongue and Korean history to maintain their national identity. Also, he emphasized the importance of Koreans marrying Koreans lest their identity be diluted. But the leader contradicted himself by marrying a European woman. This made some of his followers skeptical about his effectiveness as the president in the provisional government in exile, let alone as head of a new Korean government.

On the day Dr. Rhee and his wife arrived in Honolulu, a few of his followers went to the pier to welcome the newly married couple. At least the welcoming party was glad to see their leader happy with his new wife. Already, the depauperism of the old bachelor was gone. But the Koreans were not impressed with his Austrian wife.

The disappointed members began to withdraw their financial support for the leader. This affected the couple who had no other means of supporting themselves. Without money to buy enough groceries, Mrs. Rhee was very careful with the food she had on hand. One day a visitor found the couple washing spoiled cooked rice to eat.

Sympathetically, Young Oak took the initiative to collect donations from the members of the Comrade Society. In a few days, she raised about 200 dollars. Dr. Rhee and his wife never forgot what Young Oak did for them when they were without money and moral support. In the course of time, the Koreans forgave their leader and resumed their support for the common cause.

Throughout her longtime association with Dr. Rhee, Young Oak discovered that Dr. Rhee tended to be dictatorial in his handling of the Comrade Society. Often she was bothered by the manipulative tactics Dr. Rhee used for his own political advantage. But this didn't change her conviction about his total dedication to the independence of Korea. She believed that no other Korean leader could match Dr. Rhee's patriotism. Whenever Dr. Rhee habitually blew his finger tips, a habit he developed during the brutal torture in the Korean prison, Young Oak was reminded of his patriotic commitment.

11
UNEXPECTED DEPARTURES

By the beginning of the 1970's, Young Oak had been a widow for almost 20 years. Her sons in their 40's and 50's kept asking their mother to marry if she came across a decent man. She made some serious searches for a prospective husband, but her attempts did not produce any satisfactory results. Some of the conditions Young Oak presented were not easy ones for a widower to accept, especially among the men of Korea. For instance, she would not settle down in Korea under any circumstances. Nor did she want to be away from her sons and grandchildren in Hawaii.

In 1971 Young Oak was introduced to a Korean widower about her age. Young Oak had known his father well but not the father's son. Since he had come to Hawaii with his parents when he was little, the Korean-born widower had become considerably Americanized. He had worked as a chemist in a sugar refinery until his retirement.

The couple found each other quite compatible and were married on May 20, 1971. Young Oak was 70 years old. Her children and grandchildren were happy for the matriarch to have found a companion in her twilight years.

Even after remarriage, Young Oak retained her last name, Chung. Thus she remained legally Mrs. Chung, to which her second husband did not raise any objection. She felt that she was too much of the Chung's clan to change her last name at this stage of life.

Young Oak enjoyed the second marriage. Her husband seemed to know how to please a woman. The cheerful, outgoing man made every moment they spent together delightful. At the age of 70, Young Oak experienced new things in life that were not known to her during her first marriage with her late husband who was too strict and old-fashioned. He deliberately avoided affectionate expressions. To him, marriage was something one was obligated to do because of legal and family responsibilities. On top of this, the 27-year difference created a tremendous emotional and physical gap between husband and wife.

The newly married old couple enjoyed the high lifestyle of Honolulu. Money was not a concern to them. Young Oak's children saw to it that the old couple were not troubled for want of money.

The only regret Young Oak had about the second marriage was that she had waited so long. She wished that she had found someone as suitable as he a long time ago.

After two happy years, Young Oak began to notice that her second husband showed indifference toward her. Even worse, sometimes he didn't come home at night and wouldn't tell her where he had stayed. This was something Mrs. Chung had never experienced in her previous marriage. She did not know how to react to the situation, and she was extremely troubled by the irregularity.

As a matter of fact, Young Oak became more concerned about bringing shame upon the Chung family than losing her second husband. Thus, she didn't reveal her problem to anyone. But her sons, especially the physician, noticed physical signs of strain in their mother. The color of her hair and skin looked dull. Her radiant, cheerful smile was not there. Yet the proud mother kept her agony to herself. She was overwhelmed with the sense of shame.

One Friday afternoon, when she returned from her routine appointment at the hairdresser's, she found a letter on the kitchen table. It was from her husband. In the letter he thanked Young Oak for her love and generosity, but he had decided to end the relationship. He even suggested to her that she should not search for him.

As she looked about the house, she found that he had emptied his dresser and had taken every item that belonged to him. She realized that he really meant what he had said. Yet she could not give him up without a try. She managed to find out where he was staying. Young Oak offered unconditional forgiveness for his infidelity and appealed to him to return. But he was adamant. That was the end of her second marriage.

When she thought of her children, she felt terribly ashamed for not making the marriage a success. It was very hard for Young Oak to accept the fact that she, a 72 year-old, well-known matriarch, was divorced. She even felt guilty for not remaining loyal to her late husband. After all, she had been a widow for 20 years, and she felt that she should not have tried the second marriage in the first place.

A Lasting Monument

All of Young Oak's six sons were doing very well. As far as she could tell, they had happy homes and were prosperous in their chosen careers. Not only did the six brothers help each other, but also their affection to their mother was the envy of many Korean mothers in Honolulu. Thus their happiness and success became the source of pleasure and pride to the old mother. Some called her a "queen" because of her happy and comfortable life. Young Oak couldn't be happier with the prosperity and growth of her clan.

Of the six brothers, Robert Chung, the fourth, brought the family much of the fame and wealth. This bright son was the only one in the family who had pursued post-graduate professional training. His medical and civic services were well recognized in Honolulu.

The climax of his medical service came when Castle Memorial Hospital came into existence on the east side of Honolulu. Dr. Chung was instrumental in establishing the hospital.

There had been no hospital in the growing community of Kailua until 1963. Patients requiring hospitalization had to be transported to medical facilities in downtown Honolulu. Before the construction of the freeway connecting Kailua to Honolulu, patient transportation took 45 to 60 minutes, depending on the weather and traffic condition. Often such a distance could be a matter of life and death for emergency patients.

One day Dr. Chung was taking a woman in labor to a Honolulu hospital. By the time his car reached the peak of the hill, Dr. Chung saw the head of the baby coming out. He pulled his car to the side of the road and conducted the delivery in the car. He wrapped the baby in his coat and continued driving to the hospital. After this he felt that there should be a hospital for the Kailua community. The sincere Christian doctor began to pray for a hospital in the community he was serving.

Not long after the emergency delivery on the road side, there was an accident at a Kailua construction site. Five workers were seriously injured when a concrete floor collapsed. The inadequate emergency care was widely publicized in the press and radio.

The citizens of Honolulu, especially the east side of the city over the hill, began to realize the absolute necessity of having a hospital. But the downtown hospitals opposed the suggestion; they were concerned about the loss of patients.

But the ensuing events made the necessity of a hospital more urgent. The urgency was painfully felt by the parents of Jodi, who was only two years old when a fatal tragedy struck.

One day Jodi's mother gave her little girl a penicillin pill, but the pill blocked the child's windpipe. Instantly Jodi passed out and a member of the family applied artificial respiration. It took almost 20 minutes for an ambulance to reach Jodi's home. There were no vital signs by the time the little girl was brought to Dr. Chung.

With the father's consent, Dr. Chung opened the girl's throat and administered oxygen. Also he opened the chest and injected adrenaline into the heart and began massaging it. After 15 minutes, Jodi's heart began to respond.

Jodi was put in an ambulance with Dr. Chung riding beside her and rushed to St. Francis Hospital in downtown Honolulu. But the ambulance was carrying only a small oxygen tank, and it gave out before reaching the hospital. By the time the ambulance reached the hospital, it was too late to revive Jodi. The doctors agreed that Jodi might have been saved if she could have reached the hospital sooner. The death of Jodi troubled both citizens and government officials.

The dream of Dr. Chung for the people of Kailua came true when the 72-bed Castle Memorial Hospital was completed in January 1963. He was the first physician who saw the first patient in the hospital, a privilege given to the prime mover of the hospital project.

The hospital grew since the community it was serving was rapidly growing. It became a 150-bed hospital by 1972, thus becoming the second-busiest medical facility in the State of Hawaii. The hospital has been run according to the health principles of Dr. Chung, a faithful Seventh-day Adventist.

Dr. Chung's father did not live long enough to see the achievement of his son, Robert, yet the spirit of the old soldier patriot was evident in the son's service for the community.

Dr. Chung was not merely a busy physician. He extended his interest and service to the larger community. He became a director of the Junior Chamber of Commerce and in 1954 was voted the Outstanding Young Man of Windward. Dr. Chung also served as the Winward Oahu Community Association President.

His public services culminated when he was twice appointed Chairman of the Honolulu Police Commission. In this demanding and challenging position, Dr. Chung distinguished himself as an honest, intelligent, responsible, and energetic commissioner.

The busy young man found time and interest for the business world. He became the President of Winward Land Company, Aloha Land Company, and Cosmopolitan Land Company. He developed the Maunawili Estates area of Winward Oahu. Like his brothers, he was also involved in the running of the family business as its vice-president and treasurer.

Sudden Fall of the Rising Star

It was Sunday, May 30, 1973.

Dr. Chung was agonizing over a patient in labor with twins. He was scared that he might have to choose either the mother or her twins. There seemed to be no way to save both mother and babies.

But after many prayers and careful consultations, he was able to save them all. Dr. Chung was so happy and relieved that he decided to celebrate the successful operation in a unique way: flight. He invited the anesthesiologist's family and his wife to join him. But his own wife politely declined in order to stay home with their small children.

The twin-engine Beechcraft plane owned and piloted by Dr. Chung crashed near the Honolulu Airport as he attempted to land. The pilot and five passengers were killed instantly. The six-passenger plane was badly burned from the impact, except the tail section.

In the face of the unexpected death of their brother, the other sons became concerned about the reaction of their mother to the tragic news.   All went to their mother's home to break to her the sad news.

The mother, noticing that Robert was missing and that her sons looked grim intuited that they had come to convey sad tidings.

"Why did you all come unexpectedly?   By the way, where is Robert? Tell me what happened."

The mother felt ominous.

"Robert is gone," Ronald painfully told his mother.

When she heard of the tragic end of her son, she was calm. Collecting herself in front of her grief-stricken sons, she tried to make sense out of the tragedy.

"Life comes from God. There should be reasons for his premature death. Many mothers lost beloved sons during the war."

The mother tried to comfort her sons. Yet she could not understand why the rising star had to fall so soon. He was only 47 years old.

The mass media of Honolulu reported the tragic death of its police commission chairman as top news. The city newspapers detailed the accident and ensuing events. Many eulogized the late Dr. Robert Chung.

The Honolulu Police Chief, Francis Keala, made the following statement: "Dr. Chung's tragic death is a sad blow to the Police Department and to the community. His tireless efforts on behalf of the department and his deep dedication that the department be kept at its maximum effectiveness are well known to policemen and to the citizens of Oahu."

Feeling the big loss, Mr. Frank F. Fasi, the Mayor of Honolulu, said, "I have got to say that here is one of the best who left too early. We feel very bad about what happened, and we can't understand why some things happen the way they do happen." The mayor, who was a close family friend, added the following observation, "He was a young man, in the prime of his life, who didn't smoke, didn't drink, didn't swear; he was a real good Christian who practiced the rules and precepts, the philosophy of Christianity every day of his life. He was a good husband and father. He was a good friend. He was the kind of man who always had a smile on his lips, a good word for just about everybody. He was a great citizen, a great man, and a good Christian."

Mr. Paul Devens, the City Managing Director, said that Dr. Chung's "spiritual and civic service were so interwoven that it is not easy to separate one from the other. His keen and inquisitive mind and his golden character and desire to serve were his initial assets." Mr. Devens continued to characterize the police commissioner as a man of boundless energy. "He carried out his weighty obligations always with the ability to break a serious moment with a happy smile, almost child-like laughter and never, never a harsh word." He referred to Dr. Chung's death as a "community tragedy."

More than a thousand, including the city mayor and the police chief, attended the funeral of the late Dr. Chung.

At the funeral hundreds of the uniformed Honolulu policemen lined up to pay the last tribute to their commissioner. To the solemn playing of "Nearer to God" by the Royal Hawaii Band, the body of the former army captain was buried in the Punch Bowl National Cemetery.

The officiating pastor said, "We bury his body here, but his influence will live forever."

Dr. Chung's portrait is a permanent display in the lobby of Castle Memorial Hospital.

The Castle Memorial Hospital Board of Trustees made an official record of their appreciation of Dr. Chung's contribution. In the letter sent to his wife, they recognized the merit of Dr. Chung in these words:

> The Board of Trustees of Castle Memorial Hospital wishes to extend its grateful appreciation to the family of the late Robert C. H. Chung, M.D., for all that he has meant to this institution. Castle Memorial Hospital was conceived in the heart of Dr.

Chung; it was born through his will and nurtured by his efforts with the help of God until it became the vital force for health care delivered with Christian love that it is today in this community.

Doctor Chung's memory permeates the history of the hospital from its original fund-raising drives to the recent expansion program. His support, his interest, and his untiring efforts will long be remembered by those who carry on the service this institution was designed to render.

In honor of Doctor Chung and for the perpetuation of his memory, the Board of Trustees has voted that his portrait appropriately inscribed be placed in the board room at the hospital. His family can rightfully be proud of the contribution he has made as a staff physician and as a dedicated member of the Board of Trustees, and for this contribution we sincerely acknowledge our gratitude.

The Board of Trustees, Castle Memorial Hospital, June 1973.

The son of the plantation-worker father and the picture-bride mother left a lasting monument eloquently testifying the spirit of his parents who exemplified a life of service for their community and country.

Fall of the First Fruit

Young Oak was proud of her tall, handsome-looking Harry. He was the first fruit of her marriage to Mr. Chung Bong Woon in Hawaii.

Harry shared much of the pain and pleasure of the early years on the plantation with his mother. More than anyone in the family, Harry understood his mother's struggle with his father and the six rowdy boys. The thoughtful, sensitive first son was always sympathetic to his mother, and the mother really appreciated his compassion.

Harry and the boys were painfully aware that their mother was deprived of the joy of married life after the severe accident their father sustained. To them, their mother was a living sacrifice to her old husband and six boys. For this reason, their love and respect was almost religious.

Harry used to say to her, "Mother, I feel sorry for you not having a daughter. Your life surrounded by seven men must have been tough and rough."

From their early childhood, Mr. Chung instilled a strong sense of responsibility in the mind of Harry for his younger brothers. Mr. Chung reminded his first son constantly of the importance of setting a good example to his younger brothers in every aspect of life. Often the father punished the oldest son for his younger brothers' faults.

After World War II, Harry served in Korea for three years as a civilian technical consultant. With his brother William, he devoted his energy to the building of the growing family enterprise, the Twentieth Century Furniture Company.

His friendship with Mr. Frank Fasi resulted in the family's political debut in Honolulu politics. With Harry in charge of fund raising and campaign management, Mr. Fasi won the first mayoral election in 1968. After that Mr. Fasi won two more elections, including a surprise come-back. Were it not for a prolonged and expensive legal case, Mr. Fasi might have run for the governorship with the support of the Chung brothers. The mayor appreciated Harry's unswerving friendship and loyalty under all circumstances.

The highlight of Young Oak's life came when Harry and his brothers decided to throw a big party for their mother's 75th birthday in 1976. As many as 6,000 well-wishers, both Korean and American, came to celebrate the birthday of the matriarch of the Chung clan. When the mother entered the huge reception hall, a brand-new white Lincoln with red interior was sitting there as a birthday present.

During the ceremony, the president of the Hawaiian Mission of the Seventh-day Adventist Church briefly told the life story of the picture bride. It was a moving, remarkable success story by anyone's measure. To highlight the growth and prosperity of the Chung clan started by a 16-year old picture bride in May 1918, Reverend Davidson presented the five sons and their wives, 29 grand-children, and six great-grandchildren. All of her offsprings were doing well. Young Oak was saddened only by the absence of her husband and her fourth son, Robert.

Young Oak was shocked when she heard that Harry had a malignant brain tumor. Without delay, the doctors performed brain surgery, but Harry never regained consciousness. He died on January 16, 1982, at the age of 62 without having the chance to talk with his mother for the last time.

Sadness overwhelmed the old mother. The untimely death of Harry in his prime caused too much pain for her to deal with. For a long time, she lost her appetite. Many nights she stayed awake with an uncontrollable heartache, feeling as if half her own body and mind were gone with Harry. Her attachment to her first son was especially strong after Mr. Chung Bong Woon passed away. The first son took the place of his father in the life of his mother.

She had lost two prominent sons in 10 years. This caused her much pain. Like the Korean saying, "If a parent dies, the children bury the parent's body in the ground. But if a child dies, the parents bury the child's body in their hearts," the mother has kept the two dead sons always in her heart. Living with the memories of the two sons, she felt like a tree with two large branches broken.

By this time, she even felt guilty to have outlived her husband and two sons. If her own longevity meant facing the absence of her loved ones, she would rather die than face another death in the family.

The deaths of the dominant husband and the famous president had left a void in her life. But the unexpected departures of her two sons left her with unending sadness.

Time and again she realized the impermanency of life on this earth. Fame, wealth, and power seemed to be almost meaningless after death stung. Only the hope of the resurrection kept her from giving up.

Dr. Robert Chung with his family (above)
and with the Mayor of Honolulu, Mr. Frank F. Fasi (below).

Dr. Robert Chung (above) and
Castle Memorial Hospital in 1963 (below)

Dr. Chung Finally Gets 'His' Hospital

Adv. 1-14-63.

Happiest man in Windward Oahu yesterday probably was Dr. Robert C. H. Chung, Kailua physician, who saw the culmination of seven years of work towards a goal.

This goal was a hospital for Windward Oahu, now an accomplished reality. with the opening of Castle Memorial Hospital yesterday.

IT IS DR. CHUNG who spearheaded Windward Oahu's efforts to get a hospital.

The campaign for a hospital began under the

mer May Kirkpatrick of Richmond, Mo., and they have five children.

DR. CHUNG has been president of WOCA and a member of the Windward Oahu Chamber of Commerce, Kailua Junior Chamber of Commerce, Windward Oahu Rotary and other clubs.

For relaxation, Dr. Chung enjoys flying and playing the organ, but right now it's the Castle Memorial Hospital that is giving him his great-

Civil Defense Exercise

A Civil Defense medical exercise planned for Windward Oahu should be an attention-getter and possibly a model for other areas in the State to follow.

Dr. Robert C. H. Chung, chief of health and medical operational services for C. D. on the windward side, and his volunteer committee will start making plans after Christmas to set up a one-night medical exercise with 1,000 simulated casualties.

Dr. Chung said the exercise will be as realistic as possible — "a full-dress rehearsal" of what could happen in the event of nuclear attack.

Chung

S B 11-23-61

Sirens will sound. Mass feeding will be made available within two hours' notice. Transportation will be organized and hundreds of "injured" persons brought to a base hospital.

Windward Oahu Chamber Elects

Windward Oahu realtor B. Robert D. Y. Chung, secretary, and S. W. Tommy Tompkins, treasurer. New directors are Thomas

J. Connell Wednesday was elected president of the

Dr. Chung 'Outstanding Young Windward Man

Adv. 11-4-55

Dr. Robert C. H. Chung was named the outstanding young man of 1954 for Windward Oahu last night at a Kailua Junior Chamber of Commerce dinner in the Thailuana hotel.

A McKinley high school graduate, Dr. Chung is in the general practice of medicine in Kailua. He also is territorial and city-county physician for Kailua, Lanikai and Waimanalo.

He is active in many windward civic organizations, being a director of the Kailua Business group, the Windward Rotary Club and Civilian Defense. He is health chairman of the executive committee, Windward Oahu Community Association, Inc.

Dr. Chung also is a member of the Kailua JCC, the Kailua Community Association, the Kailua Seventh Day Adventist Church and is a member of the board of the Kailua Mission School. H is chairman of the Hospital for Windward Oahu committee.

Windward's Chung Named to Hospital, Care Commission

S B 4-22-59

Governor Quinn has withdrawn two names for which he originally sought Senate confirmation, one because the nominee resigned the post earlier and one because a change in residence makes his appointment impossible.

Dr. Theodore Tomita's nomination for re-appointment to the Territorial Advisory Commission for Hospitals and Medical Care was sent to the Senate through a clerical error.

He had resigned the post

City to Pay Dr. Chung For Care of Indigents

The City Finance Committee decided yesterday to pay Dr. Robert C. H. Chung a $51 medical bill for care for indigent patients.

The payment will be on the basis of what was termed a "moral obligation."

Dr. Chung is the regular City Physician for the Kaneohe and Kailua areas. While he was on vacation, he employed another physician to do his work for him, he said.

The $51 bill had been questioned because it was signed by the substitute doctor.

The Committee also recommended that Dr. Chung be paid $611 for medical

Newspaper clippings regarding Dr. Robert C. H. Chung

Police Commission chairman among 6 killed in air crash

Federal inquiry begins in Chung crash

By TERRY McMURRAY
Advertiser Staff Writer

Dr. Robert C. H. Chung,
Honolulu Police Commis-
sion

TUESDAY, MAY 22, 1973

By J. F. CUNNINGHAM
Advertiser Aerospace Writer

Th Wreckage of the $40,000
private plane, in which six
persons died here Sunday

Identified four of the bodies
as those of Chung, 47, physician and chairman of the
Honolulu Police Commis-
sion; Duane Brent Archer,
34, of 1008 Lunaai Place,

'...life was full of compassion,' wife say

By CHARLES TURNER
Advertiser Staff Writer

Dr. Robert C. H. Chung,
47—chairman of the Honolulu Police Commission, who
was killed in a plane crash
Sunday—was praised yes-
terday as "a man of peace"
who dedicated his life to his
community.

More than 1,000 mourners
filled every available room
at the Honolulu Central Seventh-day Adventist Church,
and some of them listened
to the service over the in-
tercom system, to pay tribute to the Kailua physician.

Dr. Chung's coffin,
draped with an American
flag, was banked by floral
tributes and two large pho-
tos of the popular medical
missionary.

ONE OF THE WRF

Friday, May 25, 1973   Honolulu Star-Bulletin   A-3

1,000 Attend Final Rites for Dr. Chung

burial slated for Thursday

Dr. Chung praised by associates

By LAUREL MURPHY
Advertiser Staff Writer

chairman Chung was much in news

Dr. Robert C. H. Chung,
48, who died yesterday
when the twin-engine plane
he was piloting crashed on
Kamehameha Highway,
was considered by City officials to have done a "con-
scientious job" as chairman
of the Police Commission.

Chung, a Kailua physi-
cian, was first appointed to
the board in August 1969, to

cause of the close relation-
ship between his brother,
Harry C. C. Chung, and
Mayor Frank F. Fasi.

HARRY CHUNG was
campaign leader and chief
money raiser for Mayor
Fasi.

Robert Chung was criti-
cized for siding too often
with the Mayor's Office on
Police Commission issues.

Newspaper clippings regarding the death
of Dr. Robert C. H. Chung

On her 75th birthday Mrs. Chung escorted by Harry Chung and
Mr. Frank F. Fasi (above) and Mrs. Chung cutting the gigantic
birthday cake amidst 6,000 well-wishers (below)

12

LAST CONVERSION

Robert's sudden departure from this world became the point of a new departure for his mother. His death brought about a turning-point in her religious life. For that matter, her social life had changed a great deal. During the mourning period, Mrs. Chung painstakingly examined her relationship with Robert. She wondered if she had shown the same preference for her brilliant son as was shown to Joseph by his father Jacob. She felt that she loved Robert as much as she did her other sons. But even if she had loved him more, Robert was never an object of jealousy for his brothers. He enjoyed abundant love and support from the family. There was no rivalry. His elder brothers were willing to sacrifice their own education and personal pleasures to support Robert's undergraduate and medical education at private colleges in California.

But there was one wish of Robert's that the mother hadn't fulfilled. It was to accept his Seventh-day Adventist faith.   While grieving over his death Young Oak was troubled a great deal by this.

Robert came across the faith by accident.   It was at Washington Intermediate School in Honolulu that one of the teachers came into the life of Robert Chung in an influential way.   Mrs. Georgia Dougan took an interest in Robert and talked with him about her faith, the Seventh-day Adventist faith.   Also, her Adventist physician husband, Dr. Dougan, got acquainted with Robert.   The couple had a great deal of influence in Robert's   decision to become a Seventh-day Adventist and later to become a physician.

After working in the emergency room at Queen's Medical Center as a student aide, the young Robert decided to pursue medicine.   Before leaving for the mainland to attend Pacific Union College in Northern California in 1942, he was baptized into the faith of the Seventh-day Adventist Church.

Another important person came into his life during his premed   study at the college.   It was May Evelyn Kirkpatrick, who was a devoted Adventist.   They were married in September 1947, while Robert was a medical student at Loma Linda University.   Thus the devout Christians he closely associated with and the Christian education he received firmly set his life in the Adventist faith.

His commitment to the faith was extraordinary.   As a boy, Robert worked odd hours to help his family.   When he brought the money he earned to his mother, he was given only lunch money.   He wanted to pay tithe out of his earnings, but this was not permitted.   Some time went by, and his mother noticed that he was losing weight.   When the mother quizzed him, Robert told her that he was using his lunch money to pay tithe.   Thereafter he was allowed to pay tithe.

As an adult, Dr. Chung retained his interest in the affairs both of his local church and the world mission field.   For many years he was a local church elder.   He diligently taught a Bible class and was on many committees, including the Executive Committee of the Hawaiian Mission of Seventh-day Adventists.

In the foreign mission field, Dr. Chung supported through personal offerings jungle chapels and schools, agricultural projects, and medical educational work in Montemorelos, Mexico; Nicaragua; Guatemala; Bugema, Africa; and Southeast Asia. On world trips in 1959 and 1964, Dr. and Mrs. Chung chose schools which had twice as many applicants as space and then asked the school to let them start an industry, a dairy, or some similar project to support additional students. One cow, for instance, sent two students to school in Bugema, Africa, for a year when the Chungs started a dairy there.

Whenever the couple found promising, intelligent native students who were potential nurses, doctors, or teachers, the Chungs never attempted to bring them to the United States. Dr. Chung said, "They are needed where they are." He was proud of the accomplishments of these young people.

Robert always had a burden to share his faith with the family, and he used to talk to his mother about his church and lifestyle. But his mother didn't pay serious attention to what her son was sincerely presenting to her. The polite mother would say, "Robert, it doesn't matter what church you are a member of so long as you believe in God. Church membership doesn't save you; what saves you is the condition of your faith." Nonetheless, Robert kept telling his mother about his belief whenever opportunity arose, but he didn't succeed in converting her.

Young Oak resisted studying Robert's faith because she did not want to sever her relationship with the Hawaii Korean Christian Church, where she had been a member for over 50 years. The bonds between her and the Comrade Society and the Hawaii Korean Church were too strong to be broken. Her entire social life revolved around those two groups and they became her life. She enjoyed mingling with the influential figures of the Korean community in

Hawaii and with the Korean government. To her, leaving the inner circle was almost like a fish leaving the pond.

During her time of grief, Mrs. Chung could not muffle the appeal of her son. "Mother, you should study my faith in the light of the Bible. Don't cover your eyes simply because my way is not familiar to you." The fact that she was not in the same faith as her son became a cause of guilt.

Finally, the mother decided to take Bible studies through a former missionary to Korea, Pastor George Munson. Within a few weeks, she confirmed the faith of Robert and accepted it.

On October 31, 1974, Mrs. Chung was baptized into the faith of the Seventh-day Adventist Church. She was born again at the age of 73, less than two years after Robert's death. Then she began to realize why Robert was so eager to share his faith.

Charity Work

The 73-year-old born-again Adventist decided to spend the rest of her life in meaningful work. So she went to Korea to sponsor a nursing home that would provide care to old people. But in a country where children were supposed to take care of their old parents, her offer to help found such an institution didn't find any urgent taker.

But she was told that many orphanages, on the other hand, were struggling financially. A former Hawaiian resident introduced Young Oak to an orphanage which had been established years before by a Hawaiian Korean she knew well. It was called Duksung Orphanage, and it had a little over 100 orphans.

When she visited the orphanage in Pusan, the children looked malnourished. The operator told her that due to a budget cut initiated by the government, he was having a hard time feeding the children. Young Oak promised to send money for three cows. Over the years, the cows multiplied and produced surplus milk, which became a source of extra income for the orphanage.

Mrs. Chung has been visiting the orphanage almost every year since 1974, and the orphans affectionately call her "Hawaii Grandma." She has invested a great amount in the institution. The money has been used for major projects, such as building expansion, kitchen renovation, the installation of a running water system, and the like. Whenever she gets unexpected monetary gifts from her children or grandchildren, she usually sends the money to the orphanage.

She also arranged the adoption of a few orphans into American families. One of the adoptions Young Oak arranged was giving her American parents a hard time. The bewildered Korean girl was constantly crying and behaving wildly. Not knowing how to handle the girl who did not speak a word of English, her adoptive parents called upon Young Oak for help. Young Oak talked to the girl on the phone. As soon as the girl heard the familiar voice of the Hawaii grandma, she calmed down. Young Oak told the girl to behave nicely to her adoptive parents. The one phone call changed her attitude, and soon the girl accepted her new American family.

Grateful to their Hawaii grandma, the children pray every morning for the longevity of their sponsor.

Hometown Church Project

Throughout her life, Young Oak has always attributed her blessings to the Christian faith she accepted when she was only seven years old. Although her hometown, Ham An, was a small inland town surrounded by high mountains and a river, the Christian churches opened up the town to the outside world.

Young Oak's encounter with American missionaries was the beginning of her American dream. Undoubtedly this prepared her to accept readily the idea of a picture marriage years later. In addition, she came to have an exposure to modern education through the church-run night school in Ham An. She became literate and enlightened through the church.

She never forgot her wish to have her own Bible and hymnal, but the poor family could not afford to buy the books. Often she had to borrow a Bible from others to read a certain portion of it and tuck it in her memory, the only means she had of cherishing the Word of God.

Young Oak decided to pay back her indebtedness to her childhood faith by building a church of her new faith in Ham An. When she conceived of the new project, there was no Seventh-day Adventist church in her home town.

She donated $15,000 to the purchase of a spacious lot and pledged another $20,000 toward the building cost. She made only two requests for her church: red brick walls and a cross to make it look unmistakably like a church at a glance. She wanted the new church to look different from other buildings.

What a meaningful monument donated by a former picture bride who had left Ham An for the want of money! This was the second church project she took a significant part in. (The first had been the building of a branch of the Hawaii Korean Church in Seoul.) At times she received less than encouraging news about the church project in Ham An, but each time she prayed to God for His intervention. Building a church without a solid local congregation was not an easy task. Nonetheless, the building was completed and dedicated on May 23, 1987. The entrance of the church displays a permanent bronze plaque inscribed as follows. "Deaconess Chung Young Oak Memorial Church. Dedicated on May 23, 1987."

On the day of the dedication of the church, Mrs. Chung and her American daughter-in-law, May (the wife of the late Dr. Robert Chung), attended as special guests of honor.

The poor picture bride left a long-lasting legacy to her home-town folks at Ham An. She was overwhelmed with

85 years of memories in Ham An and Hawaii. Although she was born into a struggling family, she was blessed with six sons, health, and wealth. Yet she took the blessings as something to share with others rather than for her own pleasure. That has been the secret of her happiness.

Mrs. Chung's last wish is a building for her own Honolulu Korean Adventist congregation. The small group has been moving from one place to another for want of their own worship place. The exorbitant real estate prices in Honolulu have been beyond their reach. But the tenacious octogenarian never gives up. She wants to see a church for her congregation in the land where she has spent 70 years of life. That will be perhaps the last project to test the faith and will of the old woman.

In the meantime, her daughter-in-law, May Chung, has continued the world-wide mission work with money her husband left. Numerous mission projects have been established in Africa, South America, Asia, and the Caribbean. Thus, through his wife's dedication, the spirit of Dr. Robert Chung is alive all over the world.

Guiding Principles

Young Oak always remembers the admonition of the Apostle Paul in the Book of Romans. She examines her own spiritual life according to her favorite Bible verses.

Let love be without hypocrisy. Abhor what is evil. Cling to what is good. Be kindly affectionate to one another with brotherly love, in honor giving preference to one another; not lagging in diligence, fervent in spirit, serving the Lord; rejoicing in hope, patient in tribulation, continuing steadfastly in prayer; distributing to the needs of the saints, given to hospitality. Bless those who persecute you; bless and do not curse. Rejoice with those who rejoice, and weep with those who weep. Be of the same mind toward one another. Do not set your mind on high things, but associate with the humble. Do not be wise in your own opinion. Repay no one evil for evil. Have regard for good things in the sight of all men. If it is possible, as much as depends on you, live peaceably with all men. Beloved, do not avenge yourselves, but rather give place to wrath; for it is written, vengeance is mine, I will repay, says the Lord. Therefore if your enemy hungers, feed him; if he thirsts, give him a drink; for in so doing you will heap coals of fire on his head.   Do not be overcome by evil, but overcome evil with good. (Romans 12:9-21)

Until a few years ago, she read the entire Bible at least once a year. In her daily prayer for her children and grandchildren, she asks for wisdom and faith, not wealth or fame. The only thing she wants to pass on to her children is the Christian faith which has held such value to her throughout her life.

In the Chung family, every special celebration, such as a birthday party, is always ended by a prayer offered in Korean by the matriarch. Most of her grandchildren and great-grandchildren do not understand her prayer, but they know that their grandma loves God as much as she loves them.

The woman who has passed through the many phases of her life in this world is preparing herself for the last passage through the gates of the new world.

Milk-cows donated for the orphans in Pusan (above) and Mrs. Chung getting bows of gratitude from the girls in the orphanage (below)

Completed church in Ham An (above) with permanent plaque reading "Deaconess Chung Young Oak Memorial Church, Dedicated on May 23, 1987,"

13

CONCLUSION AND
EPILOGUE

If "gold mountain" (as the Chinese called California and its surrounding states), "Chinatown," and the wartime "relocation camps" have been the major themes of writings on the early Chinese and Japanese immigrants in America,[1] then sugar plantations, picture marriages and the independence movement would be the major themes of the early Korean immigrants. These Korean themes are best understood against the backdrop of Hawaii whose Korean population outnumbered that of the mainland until after the Second World War.[2]

Perhaps no one is better acquainted with these three themes than Mrs. Chung Young Oak. Her life has revolved around them, and she has been a resident of Hawaii since 1918.

As one reads the history of Mrs. Chung, certain leading threads in her colorful life-tapestry are apparent. These helped to sustain her as she wove her life, and she has de-fined each life situation according to them.   In her case, they turned out to be "success factors." Therefore, identify-ing these leading threads is the key to understanding her life.

First, the family has been her most important concern. Her whole life has always been centered around it. In the beginning she decided to try picture marriage mainly to help her struggling family, especially her student brother in Japan. Otherwise she might not have ventured into marriage with a stranger in a faraway land. After her marriage to Mr. Chung Bong Woon, she was fully dedi-cated to her own family. This should not be taken for granted when considering the adverse circumstances she was in. All along she let nothing stand between her and her family's well-being.

In turn she has been enjoying the strong support of her offspring's families. Even after her husband's death and the marriages of the grown-up sons, the old matriarch has remained the pivotal center of the Chung clan symbolically and substantially. Her own good example as a faithful wife and caring mother must have been a powerful influence on her children, grandchildren, and great-grandchildren. So far, none of the Chungs over the four generations has divorced, an impressive record in the large clan.

Secondly, she has always lived with a strong sense of gratitude to her benefactors. Until this day, she is deeply grateful to her late husband who passed away almost 40 years ago. This deep sense of gratitude made her a loyal and faithful wife in spite of serious marital difficulties and also has helped her maintain rewarding, long-lasting relations with others. She has practiced the age-old Korean moral precept: "The one who fails to repay one's in-debtedness of gratitude does not deserve being called a hu-man."

Third, education is a very important asset to Mrs. Chung. She was eager to educate herself although cir-cumstances allowed only a few years of schooling at the el-

ementary level.   This educational zeal continued as she
raised her children.   For instance, the decision to move from
the familiar plantation to Honolulu, a major move, was
motivated by the desire to achieve a better education for the
children.

The emphasis on the importance of education was very
much evident among her children.   When Robert showed
academic excellence, the older brothers were united to support his expensive medical education at a private institution, Loma Linda University.   The Chungs have produced a
number of professionals, such as physicians, lawyers, and
the like.

The fourth success factor has been the Christian faith
she accepted at an early age.   That faith instilled in her a
sense of trust and optimism, which has provided her a positive outlook in life.   Although raised in a rural Korean
village where a girl would normally be expected to remain
passive and dependent, Mrs. Chung dared to dream of
something beyond the bounds of a small village.   The positive outlook kept her out of the fatalistic trap in which
many Koreans were caught in the early part of the century.

Furthermore, the positive outlook helped her convert
life crises into worthy causes.   For instance, after the death
of her husband, she became actively involved in building a
sizable church in Seoul, even against the advice of President Syngman Rhee.   The sudden deaths of the two sons
made her turn to help a struggling orphanage in Pusan
and another church building project in her hometown, Ham
An.

Also the Christian faith helped her adjust to the new
life in Hawaii.   Once she settled down in the islands, she
enjoyed the support of the Korean Christian community.
At the same time, her active involvement in the church
gave her a sense of belonging and self-worth.   Through the
church, she got involved in the independence movement,
which enlarged her social circle.

Finally, her altruistic concern expanded her horizons
and made her respectable.   The sense of public duty has led

her to get involved in many public projects, ranging from private charity to governmental campaign. It has been her philosophy to use the blessings of her life for the benefit of others. The hardships she experienced in the early years, particularly in Korea, made her sympathetic with the sufferings of others.

The story of Mrs. Chung and her clan shares some common threads with many successful Korean immigrant families in particular, and some Asian immigrant families in general. For instance, the emphasis on family solidarity and the sense of gratitude are attributed to the educational and economic success among Asian-Americans.[3] Also the homogeneity of each Asian group has made it easy to form various community organizations in the host country. These organizations, especially the Christian churches among Koreans,[4] help individuals adjust to a new environment while maintaining a sense of community and ethnic identity.

One striking aspect of her life story is the absence of any mention of negative experiences of racial prejudice.[5] Perhaps this was due to the relative isolation of the sugar plantation and her social network in Honolulu from the white community. In the later years, the Chungs enjoyed considerable reputation, associating with the upper class members of Honolulu society.

However, there is one aspect that distinguishes the Chung clan from the average Korean immigrant family. That is their early political establishment in Honolulu city politics after considerable economic success in furniture manufacturing, medical practice, and real estate investment. Undoubtedly, the older brother's association as campaign manager to Mayor Fasi helped his well-known physician brother get appointed to the Honolulu police commission and later to the powerful position of chairman. The wealth and visibility of her sons, in turn, might have helped the mother to be recognized by the Korean community and the Korean government through the Consulate General of Honolulu. She was an invited guest of every

Korean president whenever they visted Honolulu. If Robert and Harry had not died prematurely at their peak, the Chungs would have continued their upward mobility both in wealth and power. Probably the children developed their political interest through their parents, especially their mother.

When one looks at the ensuing generations, some of the characteristics of Mr. and Mrs. Chung Bong Woon are becoming less evident. For example, the strong Korean national identity and patriotism of the first-generation Chungs are not significant anymore to later generations. Assimilation through intermarriage and full-scale integration with mainstream Honolulu society made the retention of Korean identity almost impossible, even impractical. Their own social mobility required integration with the mainstream society, not isolation from it.

For this reason, the second-generation Chungs don't appear to have experienced the phenomenon of "marginal man"[6] because their economic and political bases have not been centered around the Korean community in Hawaii. As a matter of fact, the relatively harmonious multi-racial Hawaiian society has not created any exclusive and isolated ethnic ghettos. Such a society has made socio-cultural integration of various ethnic groups easy and fast.

Moreover, there is no evidence to confirm the phenomenon of "Hansen's Law"[7] among the third-generation members of the Chungs. There are no signs indicating the renewed interest in the Korean heritage of their grand-parents among them. The assimilation seems to have reached the point that their Korean cultural heritage is felt only biologically and symbolically.

The story of the poor picture bride from Ham An and her clan in Hawaii is one of the unique success stories in the history of Korean Americans.

Epilogue

Young Oak has been living alone in one of the high-rise buildings in downtown Honolulu. Her two-bedroom condominium is on the 29th floor, from which she can see much of the city, Diamond Head to the left and Pearl Harbor to the right. Her living room faces the blue Pacific Ocean, a constant reminder of the first voyage she made more than 70 years ago. Her good health, frequent telephone checks by her offspring, and personal visits make such a living arrangement work.

On her balcony, she keeps an old exercise bike. Her daily routine consists of pedaling the bike, at least ten push-ups, and a two-mile walk. When she demonstrates the push-ups, her two knees visibly bend, almost touching the floor. She takes great joy in walking to the family store to chat with her sons and others in the clan.

Her days are occupied by family affairs and church concerns. Although she is the oldest member of her church, others seek her opinions and advice on a wide range of questions. When the pastor is out of town, she speaks once in a while during the regular service.

One concern she is burdened with is the future of the family business. As the multinational corporations take over much of the tourist business in Hawaii by buying hotels and other real estate, the small independent local businesses are given fewer contracts or subcontracts. This has affected the family business considerably. Furthermore the well-educated third-generation Chungs are not much interested in taking over the business. They want to pursue their own chosen professions rather than continuing in a tough business.

Mrs. Chung doesn't understand how the American government (or for that matter the state government) lets foreign corporations take away the livelihood of citizens.

She now restricts air travel. Although she wants to make one more trip to Korea to see the church at Ham An and the orphanage in Pusan, she doubts her strength to

take such a long flight. Even the short trip to the mainland is not easy anymore. She keeps saying she might go
anytime.

NOTES

[1]Jesse Hiraoka, "Asian American Literature," in *Dictionary of Asian American History*, edited by Hung-Chan Kim (New York: Greenwood Press, 1986), p. 95.

[2]Koreans in Hawaii and on the mainland: 4,533 and 461 (10:1) in 1910; 4,950 and 1,677 (3:1) in 1920; 6,461 and 1,860 (3.5:1) in 1930; 6,851 and 1,711 (4:1) in 1940. These US census figures are reported in *Harvard Encyclopedia of American Ethnic Groups*, by Stephan Thernstrom, ed. (Cambridge: Harvard University Press, 1980), p. 602.

[3]See Hyng-Chan Kim's *Dictionary of Asian American History* (New York: Greenwood Press, 1986), p. 88.

[4]Since the first Christian service on the Mokuleia sugar plantation on the island of Oahu on July 4, 1903, the Christian church has been an integral part of the Korean immigrant community. A brief historical overview of the relationship of the two is presented in "History and Role of the Churches in the Korean American Community", *The Koreans in America 1882-1974*, compiled and edited by Hyung-Chan Kim, and Wayne Patterson, (Dobbs Ferry: Oceana Publications, Inc. 1974), pp. 124-140.

[5]Racism has been the major concern of Asian-American writers. See Elaine H. Kim, *Asian American Literature: An Introduction to the Writings and Their Social Context* (Philadelphia: Temple University Press, 1982), p. xiii. Hiraoka, op. cit., p. 95.

[6]The term "marginal man" was introduced by Robert E. Park in the 1920's. It refers to a person who experiences ambiguity by reason of belonging to two different cultures simultaneously, i.e., the home culture of one's parents and the host culture of the larger society. For this reason, the marginal man is not fully identified with either of the two groups. Such is more common among second-generation children of foreign immigrants.

[7]Marcus Lee Hansen's Law refers to the increase of ethnic interest and awareness among the grandchildren of the original immigrants. It states: "What the son wishes to forget the grandson wishes to remember."

BIBLIOGRAPHY

Ahn, Chang-ho. "A Korean Appeal to America." *The Nation*
108:2807 (April 19, 1919), pp. 638-639.

Allen, Richard C. *Korea's Syngman Rhee*. Rutland, Vt.: Charles E.
Tuttle Co. , 1960.

Cameron, Nigel. *From Bondage to Liberation: East Asia 1860-1952*.
Hong Kong: Oxford University Press, 1975.

Choe, Yong-ho. "The Early Korean Immigrants to Hawaii: A
Background History," in *Korean Immigrants in Hawaii: A
Symposium on Their Background History, Acculturation and
Public Policy Issues*. Edited by Myoungsup Shin and Daniel B.
Lee. Honolulu: University of Hawaii, 1978.

Choy, Bong Youn. *Koreans in America*. Chicago: Nelson-Hall
Inc.1979.

Clyde, Paul H. and Burton F. Beers. *A History of Western Impact
and Eastern Responses, 1830-1975*. Englewood Cliffs, NJ: Prentice
Hall,1975.

Denzin, Norman K. *The Research Act* (2nd ed.). New York: McGraw-
Hill Book Co., 1978.

Fairbank, John King (ed.). *The Chinese World Order: Traditional
China's Foreign Relations*. Cambridge: Harvard University Press,
1968.

Harney, Robert F. *Oral Testimony and Ethnic Studies*. Toronto: The
Multicultural History Society of Ontario (no date).

Kim, Elaine H. *Asian American Literature: An Introduction to the
Writings and Their Social Context*. Philadelphia: Temple
University Press, 1982.

Kim, Hyung-Chan and W. Patterson. *The Koreans in America 1888-
1974*. New York: Oceana Publications, Inc. 1974.

Kim, Hyung-Chan (ed.). *Dictionary of Asian American History*. New
York: Greenwood Press, 1986.

Melendy, Howard B. *Asians in America*. New York: G. K. Hall &
Co. 1977.

Oliver, Robert T. *Syngman Rhee: The Man Behind the Myth*. New
York: Dodd Mead Co., 1954.

Patterson, Wayne and H. Kim. *The Koreans in America*. Minneapolis: Lerner Publications Co., 1977.

Sarasohn, Eileen Sunada. *The Issei: Portrait of A Pioneer*. Palo Alto, CA: Pacific Books, 1983.

Schwartz, Howard and Jerry Jacobs. *Qualitative Sociology*. New York: The Free Press, 1979.

Song, Cathy. *Picture Bride* (poems). New Haven: Yale University Press, 1983.

Sunoo, Sonia Shinn. *Korea Kaleidoscope: Oral Histories* (vol. 1). Davis: United Presbyterian Church, 1982.

Takaki, Ronald T. *Pau Hana: Plantation Life and Labor in Hawaii*. Honolulu: University of Hawaii, 1983.

Thernstrom, Stephan (ed.). *Harvard Encyclopedia of American Ethnic Groups*. Cambridge: Harvard University Press, 1980.